10/16/

To Jim C

This is your copy!

Chet Grant

(an expression of my appreciation for your appreciation.)

C.G.

ERRATA

p. 10....we tarry as guests of a Church dignitary at Logansport before proceeding to Lafayette, which will produce another famous athletic family for Notre Dame, the Crowes.

p. 35...Edgar Allen Poe should read Edgar All<u>an</u> Poe.

Before Rockne at Notre Dame

Before Rockne at Notre Dame

Impression and Reminiscence

by

CHET GRANT

DUJARIE PRESS

NOTRE DAME INDIANA

Library of Congress Catalog Card Number: 67-24415

. . . to the strong and humble

Capt. L. L. Salmon, N. D. U.

1

I was born in 1892, the golden anniversary of the University of Notre Dame and the year to which the Gold and Blue's unbroken line of intercollegiate competition dates. Defiance, Ohio, where I was born, produced Notre Dame's most famous football family, the Millers, with whom I can say of our home town, "The Founders of Notre Dame slept here one September night in 1841 en route from their native France to their first mission in America." Once I was indifferent to the affinitive pattern of these natal coincidences in time, space and event, and I didn't see the Golden Dome until I was ten years old. But football and Notre Dame were familiar to me as far back as I can remember, as names if not always as concepts. My sensitivity to both evolved into a virtually lifelong, sometimes dynamic love affair.

In the fall of 1910 I was an eighteen-year-old sports editor and general reporter in South Bend, Indiana, when Knute Rockne enrolled at neighboring Notre Dame. His posthumously published autobiography promotes an impression, compounded by a Hollywood film adaptation, that Rockne planted the seed of Notre Dame football tradition. The head coach of Notre Dame's national college champions of 1966 understandably paid tribute to the traditional Notre Dame spirit with the remark that "it all started with Rockne." But, I have reasons to be sure, given the occasion in his lifetime to check out the fruits of collaboration and editorship, Rock would have pointed out vigorously that he had been a finder, not a founder. His forte had been the genius to make the most of what he had found—an already entrenched athletic tradition in which football had attained championship recognition the year before his advent.

It is of the generation before Rockne that I would bear personal witness in this book, from the overall perspective of a unique experience spanning three quarters of a century, including teen-age years of hero worship terminated by my graduation from high school but succeeded by a five-year interlude of mixed partisan and journalistic rapport.

From 1915 through 1950 I distributed fourteen seasons on Cartier Field among five head-coaching regimes in a variety of involved personal functions: as campus sports correspondent in 1915, as player in 1916 (when Knute Rockne was assistant football coach), again in 1920 and 1921 when Rockne was headman; as sports writer and editor in 1933 ("Hunk" Anderson, my 1920-21 teammate, was head coach); as an assistant coach from 1934 through 1940 under Elmer Layden, fullback of the Four Horsemen; finally, in 1949 and 1950, as author and publisher of a weekly newsletter to Notre Dame football buffs, reporting from an inside angle the high and low seasons of Frank Leahy's win-studded coaching career. Since 1950 I have viewed the Saturday spectacle from the perspective of occasional columnist, downtown quarterback, Monday morning mentor, press box guest, grandstand partisan and, as of now, demihistorian.

In short, I am literally a little man (5-7; 138 at last playing weight) who has been almost literally there or thereabout while Notre Dame football history has been in the making. The fact that from time to time I helped make some of it for the worse doesn't, I hope, invalidate my competence to testify in the form of impression and reminiscence. I trust, too, that my degree of P. U. (perpetual undergraduate) will not cast a shadow on the reliability of my authorship or discredit Notre Dame's academic image.

In order to clarify my concept of the tradition, I've had to dig far and deep in the past. I've also felt the need to come up with a fallacy-free definition in depth of the fundamental nature of football, specifically as it affects Notre Dame and this delver into root values, and as it should concern anybody else participatively or vicariously interested in the game and its impacts on our society.

Historically, I had to delve deeper than 1842 when Father Sorin founded the institution; even deeper than 1830 when Father Badin bought the land on which Notre Dame stands and expands today; yes, deeper by the century, down to the time of La Salle the explorer and Marquette the missionary.

These latter two men are found in the last quarter of the seventeenth century pertinently portaging between the Kankakee River near its source and the great pinhook of the St. Joseph River, not far from the sites of the future South Bend and Notre Dame. It is as precursors to Father Claude Allouez that Sieur Robert de La Salle and Père Jacques Marquette belong to the Notre Dame tradition. While Father Allouez was stationed at the site of the future Niles, Michigan, his conversion of the Potawatomis in this region would be the primary catalyst of the circumstances eventuating in the foundation of the university. One of his missions, Ste. Marie des Lacs, named after two Indiana lakes (St. Mary and St. Joseph), marked the spot in northern Indiana where Notre Dame would rise in the nineteenth century.

The Jesuits were removed from that frontier when the

British dispossessed the French. Suppression of the Society of Jesus in Europe prevented replacements. In 1830 one of the Potawatomi chiefs, Leopold Pokagon, journeyed to Detroit to petition for a priest to serve his people, who had not seen a Blackrobe for half a century. This was the next stage of events leading toward the establishment in the wilderness of an institution destined for uniqueness in the American world of higher education.

One of the priests in Detroit at the time of Chief Pokagon's embassy, the story goes, was a Father Vincent Badin. Visiting him was his brother, Father Stephen Theodore Badin, whose ordination by Archbishop John Carroll in Baltimore in 1793 distinguished him as the proto-priest of America. Assigned originally to the Kentucky mission, he returned to his native France in 1820, after having traveled an estimated 100,000 miles on the American frontier. Back in America a decade later, at the age of sixty, he remounted his horse and rode through the wilderness of southern Michigan to Pokagon's village just above the state line in the west.

Seven miles to the south in Indiana was the abandoned mission at Ste. Marie des Lacs, where Father Badin built a small chapel on the southeast slope of the smaller of the two lakes, St. Mary. The pristine beauty of the setting, not to mention a hint of divine inspiration, is said to have influenced him to purchase from public and private owners that section of land of which the lakes are still the fairest natural ornaments. His immediate concerns included a school for Indian children and an asylum for orphan boys. But when he conveyed title to the Bishop of Vincennes, in whose diocese the property was located, Father Badin also intended, according to a biographer, "that this should be the site of a great university." In 1835, overtaxed by his commitment to a parish with a fifty-mile radius, he turned over a wearing load to Father Louis DeSeille, a devout young Belgian who, beloved by the Indians he lovingly served, soon succumbed to the rigors of frontier life and died deeply mourned. To replace him the Bishop of Vincennes hastened the ordination of Benjamin-Marie Petit, a young French lawyer drawn to America by Indiana's reputation as a fruitful field for missionaries. Father Petit was as affectionately disposed toward the Indians as his predecessor had been and similarly was loved by them. When in 1838 the Potawatomis were evicted from their northern Indiana lands by government decree and military persuasion, Father Petit accompanied them down the Mississippi Valley as far as the Osage River in Missouri. There he was relieved by a Jesuit, Father Hocker, but the hardships and privations and sorrows of the exodus had been too much for the frail priest, as well as for many of his charges. He died in St. Louis at the age of twenty-seven. His and the bones of Fathers Badin and DeSeille repose at Notre Dame today.

I feel that some of the roots of the Notre Dame tradition, in the most profound and encompassing sense, should be traced to the graves of these pioneer evangelists; that the dedication and initiative of the old priest and the devotion and sacrifice of the younger ones should never be disassociated from the institutional saga that is Notre Dame's.

By virtue of his personal prestige among the whites and of the location of his village, Chief Pokagon enjoyed sanctuary in Michigan just across the state line from the deported Indiana Potawatomis. He and his people again were without a priest. But another shepherd on horseback was coming.

2

Plato's school of philosophy endured a thousand years in a gymnasium, but the term for some time has been *démodé* at Notre Dame even as the designation of an edifice generally devoted to athletic activities. Now its nominal successor, the fieldhouse, will soon bow out to an "athletic and convocation center." At the same time this traditionally he-man institution seems to be losing ground to a coeducational movement which some persons deplore as a betrayal of Notre Dame's tradition.

I offer these observations reportorially, not censoriously. In truth, I'm indebted to the confusion into which the transition toward coeducation has cast me. Perplexity has nagged me into a historical inquiry that bolsters my failing faith in the durability of Notre Dame's dedicated identity in higher education.

The Founding Father of Notre Dame had long been to me, as perhaps to others, pretty much a weathered bronze sculpture at the entrance to the quadrangle; or the name of a residence hall on campus and a street in South Bend. Now I can't think of a University of Notre Dame out of context with Father Edward Sorin. I had been equally incurious about the origin of the traditional Notre Dame spirit. When I entered Notre Dame in 1915 I don't think we had a name for the special something or other—mystique with a touch of magic—which we downtowners identified with the place and the people. For one instance, we associated varsity athletics at the university with a degree of invincibility not always statistically confirmed. This impression, it now appears, was produced by the bearing of trained athletes who competed with head and heart as well as physique.

Even the interhall athletes, similarly noted for rugged, zestful rivalries, were endowed for us by propinquity or illusion with flair and poise. The image transcended the disillusioning gall of defeat, probably because the inner Notre Damer was never licked.

My interest in the pioneer period was first activated when Notre Dame football hit a decline in the 1950's so sheer that history-conscious partisan and foe alike darkly compared it to the slump of the Roman Empire. To *Look* magazine the similitude was of the fall itself. Interpreting a run of football failure at "the football school of America" as specifically "a fall from muscular grace," *Look* hailed it as a sign of a new order of academic concern rising from the ruin of an athletic era. *Time* magazine and the Chicago *Sun-Times*, among other publications, leaped into the chorus.

Then along came new coach Ara Parseghian to yank the fallen Irish from the abyss. He inherited virtually the same personnel that had undergone a 2-7 season in 1963 as well as talent that had not realized the potential of its quantity and quality during the past decade. Parseghian was not a Notre Dame alumnus. Ironically, he took for granted a special attitude at Notre Dame which at least two of his predecessors, Notre Dame graduates, had not appealed to. The returning group, spearheaded by Captain Jim Carroll, recoiling from the ignominy of a record in 1963 unworthy of both their ability and their effort, responded to the challenge of coaching changes with a resurgence of institutional dedication. The "outsider" obviously cultivated and utilized this reawakened consciousness of the power of the traditional Notre Dame spirit, implemented it with the conventional mechanical, strategic and tactical aids to successful football coaching anywhere, and came within seconds of winning the national championship at the first try, with the same grade of playing material that had floundered for years under coaches who had neglected if they had not flouted the inspirational impact of institutional tradition on which Rockne had capitalized so colorfully and spectacularly.

Ara's only "error" has been the natural one of attributing the origin of "the spirit of Notre Dame" to the wrong man. This common misconstruction of the personal source of the "magic and mystique" spectacularized by the Fighting Irish of football is one of the most pertinent reasons for my going back to the time at Notre Dame before Rockne—first of all, to the time at Notre Dame of a nonathletic, a fighting Frenchman, the Founding Father Sorin.

In 1966, the third year of the so-called *Era of Ara*, Notre Dame won the national championship for the first time since 1949. This sensational resumption of the Victory March under new management, with the promise of more of the same to come, may presuppose de-escalation of Notre Dame's academic reputation in the view of those to whom, equating athletic decadence with academic ascendance, the football players' famine was the eggheads' feast.

Under these circumstances it should come as no shock if history repeats itself in the resurrection of the old libel of overemphasis as the reward for a coaching job excellently done. Who then will rise with the comparable eloquence of Father Charles O'Donnell to meet the challenge of a new generation of green-eyed, blue-nosed debunkers and defamers?

As Echo answers Who? let a small voice of experience report the findings of an examination of the essence of football and its involvement in the Notre Dame tradition, in conjunction with some extracts, points and angles from the pages of the university's Golden Jubilee history by Timothy E. Howard, its centennial chronicle by Father Arthur J. Hope, C.S.C., and a thin, intriguing volume of Notre Dame verse in which the reason for football is deftly rhymed by a football player.

To those who do not already have the feel of football and of the Notre Dame football tradition, or would reinforce their feeling for both, I recommend that they retrace with me, swiftly and lightly, the school's approach to taking up this hard-nose game whose nature and whose place at Notre Dame happen to be interwoven with the very web of my life. We start from the motherhouse of the Congregation of Holy Cross in LeMans, France, in August, 1841, in the company of six Holy Cross Brothers of St. Joseph; destination: Vincennes, Indiana, United States of America.

3

Crossing the Atlantic from the port of LeHavre in a packet ship, we land in New York City and make the first leg of our inland journey to Albany in a paddle wheeler. From there to Buffalo we travel in a horse-drawn barge on the Erie Canal. A small, squall-tossed Lake Erie steamer, forced more than once to put in for shelter, delivers us to Toledo, Ohio, at the mouth of the Maumee River. It is while traversing the 100-odd miles down the Maumee Valley to Fort Wayne, Indiana, that we spend a night in Defiance. The Maumee is formed at Fort Wayne by the conjunction of the St. Mary's from the south and the St. Joseph's from the north, names to augur well for our mission. From this point it is a short distance to the headwaters of the Wabash River. Pressing west and south by land and stream, possibly by canal on the final stage, we pass the site of Peru, a Wabash River port that will send to Notre Dame the brothers Bergman, football stars, and John F. O'Hara, future president of the university and cardinal of the Church. We tarry as guests of a church dignitary at Logansport, which will produce another famous athletic family for Notre Dame, the Crowes.* Twenty-four days out of New York, nine weeks from LeHavre, we reach Vincennes on a Sunday. Rest up for a few days, the bishop proposes. But Father Sorin is disposed to get going. We saddle up on Mon-

The Crowes were from Lafayette.
—C.S.

day and take a look at one property across the Wabash in Illinois. When Sorin thumbs it down, we ride out at eleven o'clock that night and at nine o'clock Tuesday morning we reach the missionary station of St. Peter's in the middle of the forest twenty-seven miles from Vincennes. This is it. The young priest sends for the Brothers and all their baggage. On Wednesday we sing the *Te Deum* and a hymn to the Queen of Apostles before the altar in the pretty but rundown little chapel of St. Peter's.

Here was a man of decision and action. Mustering from among the Brothers a weaver, a tailor, a carpenter and farmer to supplement with manual talents the spiritual and intellectual functions of the group, Father Sorin in less than a year established an elementary school, despite lingual handicaps, and a novitiate "infiltrated" by recruits from Ireland. He would have started a college in Vincennes if the bishop hadn't decreed that one college already operating there was enough for that segment of the diocese. But the bishop remembered the property in northern Indiana acquired from Father Badin, by then amounting to 900 acres by virtue of intermediate purchase of additional parcels. Father Sorin and his Brothers could have this package for their own if they but set up a college and novitiate within two years—an intimidating contract which the Fathers of Mercy had rejected earlier after exploring the site. The same foreknowledge would not have daunted Father Sorin. But his strategic sense warned him against displaying too quickly or baldly his ready eagerness to embrace the challenge, lest the bishop be tempted to impose further conditions. Moreover, the Brothers were happy with their life at St. Peter's and the progress made there, especially since it had been praised by His Excellency. After two days of discussion and prayer it was agreed that the Holy Cross men still wanted to build a college. It couldn't be done by sitting on the ball or by punting to the bishop.

On the sixteenth of November, 1842, Father Sorin and seven of his fifteen Brothers loaded an oxcart and hit the line in the teeth of unseasonable inclemency; wind, snow and cold so bitter that the travelers made but five miles the first day. This was the overture to a winter which the almanac recorded as the coldest since 1607; fifteen inches of snow fell as far south as Georgia.

After eleven freezing days they arrived in the town of South Bend and were welcomed by Alexis Coquillard, the fur trader. Against his dissuasive counsel they crossed the ice-locked St. Joseph River the same afternoon of their arrival and, guided by Coquillard's teen-age nephew and namesake (who would be the first Notre Dame scholar), made their way to Father Badin's rude chapel. Two miles to the north, it looked down on a frozen little lake carpeted with snow and framed by snow-mantled evergreen trees—forming what Father Sorin described as a "delightful solitude." Writing in retrospect several years after the event, he revealed that on the occasion of this virgin view and exploration at Ste. Marie des Lacs, "special consecration was made to the blessed Mother of Jesus, not only of the land that was to be called by her name, but also of the institution that was to be founded here."

(Up to the twenties, Notre Dame teams were mainly called the Notre Dames, Notre Damers and South Benders, but most often were known by their colors, the Gold and Blue, which are the colors of the patron Lady, represented on the Notre Dame seal or coat of arms by a cross of gold on a blue field. Silver waves at the bottom commemorate the lakeside locus of the university at the founding. A silver star at the left of the gold cross is another symbol of the Blessed Virgin, Star of the Sea. In front is an open book, signifying an institution of learning. The inscription—*Vita, Dulcedo, Spes* from the *Salve Regina*—Our Life, Our Sweetness, Our Hope—links with the concern the Founder would evince for the rounded development of Notre Dame's students. The Fighting Irish moniker [spawn of the twenties] influences many to think of green as the school color. The contrasting impact of Polish names in the lineup has suggested Greenski as an ethnic variation! Do you call us the Blue and Gold? For the right sequence envision the gold of the Dome and the statue of Mary against the blue of the sky.)

After the Brothers had cleared the ground and hauled the timbers for a larger chapel, neighbors helped raise the walls, but when the cold routed them, the roof had to wait until the Bishop of Vincennes could honor Father Sorin's request to send on the Brothers who had been left behind at St. Peter's.

In early February, headed by forty-five-year-old Brother Vincent, weaver and teacher, they pointed north with a wagon heavily laden with beds, pots, pans, kitchen utensils, tools and food, and drawn by a team of four horses. They brought also eight head of cattle. Poorly shod draft animals slipped and slid on ice-filmed roads. Losing traction on a hill, they skidded to the bottom. The help of neighboring settlers was required to boost load and horsepower up the hill again and over the top. A flatboat had to be bought in order to cross a stream too deep to ford. From this the milling stock plunged into the icy water one by one and swam this way and that until all managed to end up on the wrong side of the water. Two nights were spent in the open. Bread was sliced with an ax. A wheel gave way and a day was lost. The Brothers pressed on with a large sled, piled with all their effects including the three-wheeled wagon. There were frozen toes and frozen faces by the time they reached Notre Dame on February 27, 1843, on Mardi Gras.

Obviously this ordeal was something less epical than a South African *vortrek*, a covered-wagon migration to California or a Klondike rush. But the spirit of the men, some not more than boys, was equal to more spectacular challenges. Appropriately, they had scarcely defrosted before Father Sorin brought the roofless new chapel to their attention. The next day all set to work. On March 19, 1843 (St. Joseph's Day "by blessed coincidence"), the first Mass in the new chapel was celebrated.

A veritable city of religious, administrative, academic, athletic and social edifices has arisen on the site of the wigwams and fires of the worshiping Potawatomis at Ste. Marie des Lacs. Tables for royalty can be set where the Brothers of St. Joseph were delighted that first Fat Tuesday to rate bowls of warm soup. Sleek black limousines riding in cushioned elegance on bumpless roads replace the oxcart, horseback and shank's mare that transported the Founders over many a muddy, rutted mile. Today Notre Dame claims the biggest college library building in the world and in another year will move its athletic department into a brand new athletic and convocation center with two domes. Is it relatively less impressive that by 1844 Father Sorin had his chapel, novitiate, college and a charter granted by the State of Indiana, chiefly by the sweat of a few dedicated brows?

For many years Notre Dame's nineteenth-century history was a blank area in my life. Appreciative and admiring references to the pioneer struggle left me cold—a frontier with no Indians to fight suggested tinder-dry reading for one whose youthful taste had been affected by the Jesuits among the

Iroquois, the fictional Liberty Boys of '76, Buffalo Bill and Young Wild West. But when I finally got around to the Sorin story, the aging process had prepared me to find exciting drama in any kind of struggle against tough odds, such as the daily routine of pioneering Notre Dame from the beginning.

To make space for the community the Brothers literally chop space out of the virgin woods. They build the first college structure out of their own marl beds, with bricks baked in the community kiln and laid by its members. With only this small all-purpose college building to go on, Father Sorin obtains a charter for a university. Just to have tried for it would be sufficient witness to the boldness of his vision and the aggressiveness of his leaderhip. Before he left France he adopted America and spent the rest of his life adapting himself, his associates and his procedures to this commitment, as at St. Peter's, where he preached his first sermon in alien English. . . . Americanization complicates his relations with Father Moreau, Superior General of the Congregation resident in LeMans. Father Sorin sends Father Moreau's nephew back to France because he persists in thinking like a Frenchman about Notre Dame in America. The conflict between the sense of his duty to Notre Dame and the acknowledgement of his bond to the motherhouse is a cross Father Sorin bears until he himself is elected Superior General of the order. Meantime there have been the language barriers to overcome, ethnic attitudes of the Irish members of the community to reconcile with the French approach, economic crises that incur short rations without reference to national background, countless complex real-estate maneuvers to execute that are vital to progress or even continued existence, recurrent fires and the perpetual menace of fire to be suffered; a plague that takes the lives of Fathers, Brothers, Sisters and a seminarian, twenty-two in all, and almost closes the school; climaxing his misunderstandings with the motherhouse, a showdown that almost loses the Founding Father to a bishopric in India; a national financial panic that overstrains Notre Dame's ever-fragile resources; American Civil War and a need for Catholic chaplains to which the president of Notre Dame responds with key members of the faculty.

Again and again the project is expanded when just the question of its survival might invite fearful speculation. In this American boarding school for male youth, founded and promoted by a fighting Frenchman, increasingly administered by fighting Irishmen, defeat and disillusion, disappointment and delay are only springboards for new effort and often greater return. In all this we find the developing tradition of the Notre Dame spirit as it has been dramatized in athletic competition: most forcefully and spectacularly by American-type varsity football, which became the most representative sport in this hard-driving environment by process of natural selection.

Leadership and the *esprit de corps* of the community received their greatest test by holocaust in 1879. One morning in April someone yelled, "Fire!" The main college building, dedicated in 1866—160 feet long, 80 feet wide, 90 feet (six stories) high, crowned with a dome—was soon gutted, along with some auxiliary buildings. The *Scholastic* comprehended the magnitude of the disaster with a trenchantly laconic lead phrase: "Fire, flames, ashes!"

Father Sorin, who had advanced in the Congregation of Holy Cross from Provincial to Superior General, but still regarded Notre Dame as his No. 1 ward, was in Montreal about to sail for Europe. Returning posthaste, he found the heart of the university in ruins and the community in despair. What he said then has often been quoted. "If it were ALL gone," he said, "I should not give up." The fallen bricks of the main building were still warm, it was said, as he wheeled away the first barrow to launch a rebuilding program headed by Father Corby, the president, Notre Dame's most renowned Civil War chaplain.

I understood that Ara Parseghian displayed the word "PRIDE" boldly on the walls of the dressing room in the Notre Dame stadium in 1964, the year of his dynamic and victorious debut as head coach. If this was an appeal to the "Notre Dame spirit" it was mistakenly directed. Love and loyalty are the essence of the traditional attitude toward the institution. A traditionalist would have recommended a classic rhetorical substitute for Ara's reliance, obviously inadvertent, on a sin of the intellect. More apropos of Notre Dame's doctrinal and historic commitment would be the blown-up and framed legend of Father Sorin's pledge to Notre Dame after the Great Fire, translatable in effect to the familiar generalization, "We may be down, but we're never out!" His own words could be exploited as a continuing source of inspiration and a lesson in the strength of humility, a timeless reminder that there would be no Notre Dame but for the indomitable will and toil of the Founder (Refounder, too!) and his breed.

Father Thomas J. Walsh would be the president identified with the introduction of varsity football, American style, to Notre Dame. At the time of the Great Fire he was vice-president and director of studies. All records had been lost. We are told that he reorganized classes, found spaces for them that fall in a hardly rebuilt structure, and made out schedules for professors "with nothing to guide him but his prodigious memory and eminent good sense."

Born in Canada and educated there and in France, he was a favorite protégé of Superior General Sorin. Succeeding to the presidency in 1881, he was only forty years old when he died in office, after serving twelve consecutive years. His tenure was distinguished by cultural as well as physical expansion worthy of the special gifts attributed to him as priest, philosopher, educator, administrator and social being.

We read that he liked to recline under a tree with the *Pensées* of Pascal or Bossuet's *Histoire des Variations*. But his nineteenth-century taste in philosophy and mathematics did not exclude from his presidential concern less intellectual pursuits, activities and commitments. One wonders if a certain recent lay historian failed to accord Father Thomas Walsh even honorable mention in order to avoid having to record recognition of the luster reflected on his times by the sixth and, next to Father Sorin, the youngest of Notre Dame's presidents. In any case, it was during his gracious, scholarly, firmly administered incumbency that American football came to Notre Dame to stay.

4

The Founding Father of Notre Dame has been described as an expert marble shooter who enjoyed competing with his elementary students. This apparently was his closest approach to athletic participation. But he recognized the urgency of catering to matter and emotion as well as to soul and mind. The earliest advertisement for students (1843) stressed "facilities for recreation and physical exercise." During the earlier years the major recreational resorts were impromptu wrestling, tag games, fishing, hunting, boating, tramping the woods and riverbanks of the region, with perhaps minority downtown diversions for seniors. During the 1860's some students took up such group games as baseball and soccer.

The Golden Jubilee history, its publication delayed until 1895 by Father Sorin's failing health and his death in 1893, allocates several pages to nineteenth-century recreation. Regularly organized boating clubs were first formed in the sixties. Regattas featured the annual commencement exercises. The boats, if not the crews, were pronounced "equal to the best in the land." Cup winners bore historic or poetic names like Santa Maria, Pinta, Minnehaha, Hiawatha. The Santa Maria in 1870 won the first race of record. The woods and prairies in which Notre Dame was growing harbored bear, wolf, deer, turkey, 'coon, 'possum, catamount and prairie hen. Student sons of Potawatomi chiefs or of distinguished braves often led the hunting. Among them was Simon Pokagon, son of Leopold, who would continue his education at Oberlin College, Ohio, and become regionally renowned as poet and orator and the Midwest voice of the red man. Lakes and streams around Notre Dame teemed with wild geese and "other aquatic game" when Simon Pokagon was at Notre Dame, the Golden Jubilee history notes. It recounts an encounter with more formidable game. The white boys were understandably impressed when the Indian boys with them smoked Sweet Tooth the bear out of a bee tree and dispatched him. Wednesday (later Thursday) was set aside as Recreation (Rec) Day, making possible all-day midweek walks, beginning after breakfast. Packing their baskets with staples, the ramblers relied on neighborhood farmers for fresh milk, eggs and butter. Having given a week's notice, a group might descend on a selected farmhouse to feast on "chicken, hot pies and other edibles normally exotic to their boarding school table." At least as late as 1916 an excursion to the "Pie House" on the Niles highway was a mandate on a new arrival. I remember this.

The Golden Jubilee historian was the Honorable Timothy E. Howard of South Bend, Civil War veteran, dean emeritus of the Notre Dame Law School, Chief Justice of the Supreme Court of Indiana, and one of the few members of the faculty to receive Notre Dame's highest award to laymen, the Laetare Medal.

From the first, Justice Howard wrote, the students were separated into divisions according to age: over sixteen, seniors; between twelve and sixteen, juniors; under twelve, minims. Each group had its own study room, dining room and dormitory. The author cites a more recent group known as the Sorins, pursuing more advanced studies and domiciled in new

Sorin Hall, a residential accommodation with private rooms, sponsored and promoted by Father Thomas Walsh in the late 1880's, in violent conflict with tradition. At first they shared the seniors' facilities, but, Justice Howard points out, "the grounds were found too confined after the introduction of the noble game of baseball, and a large campus was set aside for each division, some twenty-five or thirty acres now (1895) being devoted to this purpose, giving ample room for extended walks and for all the manly sports, including, alas, the redoubtable game of football. It must be said, however, that this last game has not been played at Notre Dame with the barbarous accompaniments found in too many schools and colleges. As in everything else, so in her games, Notre Dame seeks to present the best. The strong limbs, ruddy complexions and general good health of her students give evidence that her efforts in this matter have not been without success."

In the following paragraph, the Jubilee historian indicates the scope and balance of Notre Dame's educational philosophy in the Founder's time:

"For cold, wet and stormy weather all rational indoor amusements are provided. In addition to these are the libraries, reading rooms, societies, musical and dramatic entertainments, with frequent lectures, readings, concerts, etc. A feature of all these amusements and entertainments, and even of the manly sports, is that care is taken that they serve the purpose of higher education, whether physical, mental or moral. Man's threefold nature is everywhere and in everything recognized, and in the education given, body, mind and soul are always kept in view. That the physical man should grow in strength, grace and beauty; his intellect, in knowledge and wisdom; and his heart, in virtue, are deemed essential toward attaining a complete education."

A sports writer, given a forum in the *Saturday Evening Post*, described modern college football as "a game created in the name of higher education to furnish recreation and relaxation from academic pressures." He charged that "college football has grown away from original intent and purpose to become a gladiatorial spectacle for a few carefully recruited specialists."

Let's see, for controversial example, how football began at Notre Dame, so-called "Football School of America" and "Football Factory," and who it was that first publicized the need of a coach.

First of all, the introduction of football in 1887 was received by higher authority, if Justice Howard's "alas" was any tip-off, with rueful acquiescence to undergraduate initiative. Two former Notre Dame students, transfers to Michigan, promoted an arrangement whereby a Wolverine team indoctrinated an already existing soccer team at Notre Dame in the rules and performance of American football, together with a lesson in the frustrations of defeat and a demonstrated formula for victory. We read that Father Thomas Walsh "thanked the Ann Arbor team for their visit, and assured them of the cordial reception they would always receive at Notre Dame." The grace with which this induction was recognized did not necessarily connote an unalloyed presidential blessing.

Only five games were played from 1887 through 1889. Three were lost, all to the preceptors from Michigan by the respective scores of 8-0, 26-0, 10-4 (the last reverse involving a disputed decision by a Michigan player serving as referee). In 1888 Notre Dame beat Harvard School of Chicago 20-0 and in 1889 took Northwestern 9-0. Following a truce of two years, representative football in 1892 was resumed for keeps. The players evidenced an innate desire to win. Without it, a game designed to be competitive would degenerate into mere exercise, like walking for health or passive pleasure. It was a student, not a school administrator or member of the faculty, who publicly recognized victory as the name of the game and cited the inadequacy of self-directed effort, however devoted, for perfection of individual and team proficiency. An editor of the Notre Dame *Scholastic* soon was moved to write, "The players are strong and willing, but they need a coacher to teach the individuals how to unite mind, body and spirit in the common cause: how to play with and for each other to the best interest of the team."

5

The *Post* pundit's statements, of course, must be regarded as mere postulations, ignoring the very nature of football and its appeal to both participant and spectator. To create is to cause to come into existence. The reason for being of football has no essential relationship with higher education or academic pressures, patronage or hired coaching. Its vital inspiration is the primordial urge of some animals to bang each other around, group vs. group, for fun. The gladiatorial spectacle just grew—out of such natural forces as the competitive drive of man, his individual desire to excel, the inevitable division of individuals and groups into classes by rule of competence, and then the joy that nonparticipants derive from vicarious participation.

Some boys would play football if there weren't an adult on earth. They would practice and compete to outdo their opponents. With the same instinct and will to win they would seek instruction from someone in their youth bracket with more skill and experience. This spirit was recognized in a papal encyclical *Invicti Athletae Christi*, 1957. The notably intellectual Pope Pius XII (recipient of an honorary degree from Notre Dame as Cardinal Pacelli) did not exclude football, I'm sure, when, in context with a statement of the place and functions of athletics in Catholic education, he defined their purpose as "the use, the development, the control—by means of and for the service of man—of the energies enclosed in his body; the joy that comes from this power is not unlike that which the artist experiences when he is using—and is the master of—his instrument."

The artist, whatever his outlet, pursues his particular commitment under aesthetic compulsion, his love for his chosen medium of expression. Painter, musician, sculptor or poet will endure for his art's sake the most severe trials, reversals and privations. In football, in the process of activating his athletic capacity, the athlete-artist has to expose himself to physical abuse, even incapacitation. The principle is the same. He takes these risks for love of the rough kind of game football is. He welcomes the challenge and hazards of bodily contact, not for a masochistic thrill but as a condition of the game that strongly moves him to leave no effort undone in building up and refining his strength, skill and wit for the combat.

Going right along with him is the ardent spectator, training his powers of observation and appreciation, as does the spectator-lover of the fine arts, so that he may participate vicariously in the test of power, speed, technique, strategy and tactics on the field. A substantial fraction of football's huge following is following the crowd, no doubt, and another sizable segment consists of those who must be where the action is. But the essential popularity of the spectacle is the spectator's desire and faculty to identify himself with the actors, and the action. The observer becomes the observed; his intellectual and spiritual identification is as real to him as the physical prototype.

It was somewhat in this mode, perhaps, that a South Bend newspaper writer described Notre Dame's earliest intercollegiate victory, in an era when football was played and viewed more purely for its own sake than now, when so many attend the games because so many others have established the fashion to do so.

"The first 'inning' of this meeting with Albion (Michigan) College, in 1893, was scoreless. Likewise for 25 minutes of the second inning (half)," the reporter continues, "did the contest rage without scoring"—except for a two-point safety counting for Notre Dame. Only in the closing paragraph does he reveal that the final score was 8-0 in Notre Dame's favor, a vital statistic that would be displayed in today's headline and confirmed in the lead paragraph. This upside-down reporting contains a lesson in the fundamental nature and appeal of the game. The nineteenth-century reporter had been most impressed by the pattern and zest of the action. The marginal score was anticlimactic except as it served to define that particular contest.

This point of view emphasizes the recreation of both players and onlookers, the dual intent of spectator sport. From this angle the primary purpose and function of winning and losing or tying are to give definition to both the action on the field and the reaction on the sidelines. This interpretation of the significance of the outcome of a game may seem to vitiate incentive by stigmatizing the desire to win and derogating strong measures to achieve victory. On the contrary, severe training and strenuous striving to prevail are essential to the attainment of pleasure-producing proficiency in individual and team performance. In that mood, victory as well as defeat has its sting, since the end of the game, whoever wins, also terminates the occasion and source of both participative and vicarious enjoyment—just as the last curtain on a first-rate theatrical performance alloys satisfaction with regret; the better the show has been, the deeper our sighs and the greater our reluctance to take leave of the illusion that so delightfully engrossed us.

Too many of our higher educators in the age of the Big Gate appear to suffer from a guilt complex, as if large paid attendance automatically, inherently constitutes a form of bribery intended to blind them to the moral menace of intercollegiate football's immense popularity. They would be more realistic, they would spare themselves much gratuitous travail and the persons identified with the game much unwarranted censure, by thinking of football as a theatrical production. What, for one example, is a football head coach if he isn't a stage manager? The rounded football coach is organizer, administrator, pedagogue, strategist, tactician, raconteur, orator, slave driver, all rolled into one person and he may be something of a poet to boot—like Rockne when he described the precisely tailored execution of the famous Notre Dame shift with the feeling and imagination of a writer transposing the rhythms of motion into lyric language.

If Dan Casey, place-kicking guard and captain of the 1895 team, had gone into coaching, he may not have qualified strictly as a poet, but he would have been competent to express in prosodic form Justice Howard's interpretation of Notre Dame's threefold educational commitment, judging by some of Dan's undergraduate exercises that have come to my attention.

The study of verse always was part of the Notre Dame method of teaching English, the foreword to a 1917 anthology of Notre Dame verse informs us. This I might never have known had I not met Speer Strahan one spring day in 1917, while tramping the woods near Notre Dame because Father Tom Crumley (English I, the year before) had stirred in my prosaic heart a spark of cultural interest in nature. Speer

Strahan, campus poet laureate, had collaborated with a faculty member, Father Charles O'Donnell, poet, orator, and future president of the university, in making a collection of poetry and verse that had been published in the *Scholastic*, much of it the product of class assignment. Learning that Speer was a fan of Omar Khayyám, I gave him the special edition of the *Rubaiyat* I carried in my pocket. When the anthology came off the press a little later, he sent me an autographed copy.

Twelve per cent of the selected authors were athletes, mostly football players, contributing a similar proportion of the carefully culled contents, topped in number by Daniel Vincent Casey. Taken together, his three selections are seen to comprise, if a perhaps whimsical taste is allowable, a trilogy representing Notre Dame's triune educational tradition, as presented in prose by Justice Howard.

First, this bit of academic irony, a four-line exercise in iambic pentameter:

> Old books, old wood, old wine to make one glad,
> Old friends to cheer one when the raven croaks.
> I've wondered, oft, King Francis did not add,
> Eyeing his jester, "And for mirth, old jokes."

For the spiritual dimension, a Spenserian sonnet:

ASH WEDNESDAY

> Signed with the ashes of the palms we bore,
> A short time since, we bow in sudden shame
> Before Thine Altar, Lord, whose other name
> Is Mercy, while the heart weeps, crushed and sore.
> Mindful of promises we made of yore,
> That were but chaff in passion's furnace flame,
> We falter when our ready lips would frame
> Words for a sorrow never felt before.

Broken our vows, our high resolves betrayed
Because our pride was greater than we knew,
With empty hands and hearts of grief we kneel
Low at Thy Mercy Seat. We asked not aid
But trusted blindly in a strength untrue—
Our only solace is the pain we feel.

Finally:

TO MY FOOTBALL SUIT

Farewells I've spoken
And fond ties broken,
But, by this token,
  O canvas mine,
My best endeavor
Is vain to sever
I find, for ever,
  This bond of thine!

Oft have I worn thee,
Long would I mourn thee
If fate had torn thee
  And me apart.
Though stains deface thee
They do but grace thee,
Nought can replace thee
  In my fond heart.

Thy seams are ragged,
Thine edges jagged,
Thy knees are bagged
  Thy rents, a score;
But thou are dearer,
Thy beauties clearer,
My love sincerer
  Than e'er before.

Thou'rt rather muddy,
A trifle bloody,
Thou'rt quite a study,
  In gray and red;
But gold can't buy thee,
Or ragman eye thee
Or soap come nigh thee,
  Till love is dead.

Whether Casey's fondness for a discarded football suit was genuine or academic, the sentiment of his "poem," call it doggerel if you like, symbolizes a valid affection for the game which is the basic reason why boys and men risk getting their heads bashed, their teeth knocked this way and that or out, their flesh gashed and bruised, their bones broken. Without love of the game a football player would never play long enough to qualify him for professional pay. Character building is an obvious and important but not guaranteed potential of the incidence, which is dependent on contextual factors, fundamental among them the degree of the player's self-commitment. I think American football could have been included when Pope John XXIII, as of May, 1962, praised athletic competitions for fostering international brotherhood. Certainly, character would benefit from the humanistic participation the Pope had in mind when he said: ". . . sound athletics contain in themselves the aspirations which have deep roots in the hearts of men and peoples [and] contribute to the higher ideals of interior beauty and perfection, of self-control and principle, in the spirit of mutual competition which contributes to universal brotherhood and concord among nations."

An apologia for college football, more militant because of the specific identification of the subject with competition, was eloquently projected by Notre Dame's poet-president after Notre Dame had won two straight national championships (1929-1930) under Rockne. Notre Dame, among other colleges successful in football, was under the fire of the Carnegie Foundation, charged with promoting athletics with an emphasis incompatible with academic standards.

College, Father Charles O'Donnell said in part, is more than a school. It is a life:

> . . . It is a school life, of course, and the major emphasis is, as it ought to be, on study. But even if it were not, even if football ran away with one quarter of the year, there are so many worse things that could happen to a school if that healthy outlet of young energy and enthusiasm were closed. . . . Man is not all mind; he is a creature of flesh and blood; he has a heart, and the heart, too, must be schooled in a curriculum which life itself supplies in those four years crowded with wonder that make up the college career of the student today . . . Two and two make four, and the college student will learn the lesson through whatever complexities the formula may be extended. But there is another mathematics, a madder, wilder learning, more divine and nearer the source of the truth . . . It is that lesson which the heart learns of life itself . . . it is dedication and consecration of self to an ideal and a cause, even though in the particular premises that cause is only the elementary one of winning a football game for the sake of the school.

He described then the spirit of football players competing in company: retaining their individualism, yet subserving it, without subservience, to the common purpose. These athletes belong in a realm, he said, where, "forever living, dwell the custodians and the exemplars of our human heritage of valor and virtue—Sparta is there and Rome is there, Richard and

Raymond and Godfrey, the Kings of Arthur's Table, and the great Gaels of Ireland—'the men that God made mad, for all their wars were merry, and all their songs were sad'—while high and clear above that fabled and historic host rings the tocsin of federated fighting men everywhere—'All for one, one for all'."

I doubt that Notre Dame's greatest football stars have identified themselves with the Round Table knights, or crusaders like Richard the Lionhearted and Raymond, or Godfrey the Protector; or Cuchulain of the Red Branch Knights of Ancient Eire. Allow for poetic fervor and hyperbole. But there's no secret that Notre Dame teams have been acclaimed by two generations of Americans for their distinctive spirit: that incorporeal stuff lighter than gossamer, stronger and more resilient than the toughest coiled steel spring; that contagious exuberance of disciplined and schooled *esprit de corps* without which no group enterprise of consequence can succeed in fair competition—as in football, war or a marketing campaign. Fact and fancy are not so far apart when you recall the old-time Notre Dame-Army donnybrooks-with-rules in which both sides gloried. Right now millions of football followers participate with vicarious zest in a renewal of traditional Notre Dame morale, after an eight-year depression that threatened to displace the *Victory March* permanently with a dirge.

The particular cause that invokes the warrior spirit at Notre Dame was the subject of another selection from the O'Donnell-Strahan anthology. The following stanzas were written by George N. Shuster ('15) some fifty years ago. Dr. Shuster is now assistant to the president, having returned to Notre Dame after his retirement as long-time president of Hunter College, New York City.

She stands in the voiceless moonlight,
   In the misty morning dew;
She stands in the sinewy noontide
   And when the dusk falls, blue.

Her smile is a mother's yearning,
   For the sons at her white breast;
Her arms bear countless treasures
   For the lone, disquiet guest.

In study's happy sanctum,
   At games robust and bold,
We know thou art our patron,
   O Lady robed in gold.

It's common knowledge that Notre Dame athletes attend Mass in a group whenever possible the morning of an athletic event. Individually or collectively they recite the "Hail Mary" habitually and expediently. Non-Catholic members of the squad are known to join in the petition to Mary to pray for us now and at the hour of our death. There was a time when I regarded only a contingent supernatural assist toward victory as competitively unfair to our opponents. It has occurred to me since that this attitude is bigoted, denying to our opponents the same privilege and option to pray to the same Power through the same intercessor.

6

I saw my first football game in 1901, when I was nine years old: Defiance High School vs. Paulding High School; or maybe it was Napoleon—no matter. A certain play is the thing I wish to recall. The gridiron was bounded on the east and north sides by maple-colonnaded streets, everything still green, foliage and grass, the turf of the field unscuffed. It had to be an early game. The rooters in the main stood along the west side of the field. On the east side opposite, alone, far from the distractive crowd, one small boy (a baby-face with brown eyes, mop of straight black hair under a dark gray cap, wearing orange and black jersey, short pants with bottoms curling under his knees, long black stockings, high laced shoes), with no vision for anything but the action on the playing field. His mind is open to a blank page for an indelible impression of the primitive nature of football.

I still see small Tommy Gorman, the grocer's son, long, black, curly hair hidden under a round headguard, breaking out of a typical nineteenth-century midfield melee and scooting goalward, all by himself, but not for long. Immediately I sense his jeopardy, despite his good start, as a taller, lither figure leaps out of the mob, his uninhibited tawny locks streaming as he devours the ground with spring-coiled stride.

I respond to the elemental appeal of the spectacle with every fiber of my being, without consciously recognizing the analogy of pursuit and evasion which in wild nature would climax in the kill or split-second survival. In football, played by and for humans, the brute instinct is modified by certain rational values and the game is shaped by corresponding rules into Pius XII's rugged art.

Run, Tommy, run!

Chubby legs churn, but the legs of the pursued are too short. The pursuer overtakes him ten yards this side of the goal line, brings him down with lunging tackle from the rear, for which the only technique is possession and exercise of the guts to make the attempt with head up and eyes open.

I still agree with my father's and uncle's belief that the best all-around game for vigorous young men and boys, with the appropriate talent and desire, could be baseball. But I have never quite recovered from the impact of the sequence I've just described. I recall neither the immediately following events nor the ultimate result. But before that day was over that drama of pursuit to the kill was duplicated precisely by the same persons under precisely the same conditions of scrimmage, breakaway, chase and trailing tackle—as if to etch in my young mind by example a fundamental concept of the thrill in football for both player and fan.

Baseball was the family game, but as long as I can remember I was football-conscious and Princeton was my favorite, although Poe is the only player's name that sticks; perhaps because of association with Edgar Allen Poe's *Raven*, of which my mother had a special edition. There were four Poe brothers; related to the poet, by the way. I'm sure I took notice when Arthur Poe kicked a 5-point field goal in the last seconds to slip past Yale, 11-10. I had other reasons to dramatize the Tigers in my memory. I've mentioned my sweater. Horizontally striped with the colors of Old Nassau, it served

Allan – I knew this, but missed the error until called to me attention by an old friend + baseball teammate (a retired Doubleday senior Editor!

the accouchement of our cat Rosy O'Grady when her litter included a freak that lived long enough to sport the orange and black of a jungle tiger and qualify as a prospective Princeton mascot or as an exhibit in Ringling Brothers' sideshow. I do not mean that I wasn't conscious of Notre Dame during this period—on the contrary, it was a household word, but not at the time identified with football so far as I was concerned.

Nor would I have known what to make of it if someone had mentioned then that Notre Dame was ahead of its time in its requirements for law students. But I did know that Tim Ansberry, lawyer, U. S. Congressman and boyhood friend of my father was a Notre Dame man. Then, about 1896, Uncle Angus Grant went to South Bend, Indiana, to play baseball with the Greenstockings and to meet the Notre Dame athletic director and coach, Frank Hering. I didn't learn until many years later that Hering, intrigued by my uncle's stocky build, agility and wit, tried to recruit him for the Notre Dame football team. My mother, born and bred Methodist, always understood that Notre Dame was a "good school for boys." While Uncle Angus went on to play in the Southern League and American Association, my father took over the management of the Greenstockings and I heard about Angus McDonald, Notre Dame baseball star who played some first base for the Greens under my father, whether *sub rosa* I never knew. To my baseball father and uncle, football was a barbarian sport.

Francis E. Hering was Notre Dame's first full-time football coach—preceded in 1894 and 1895 only by two incumbents of slight and passing impact. Hering had won football letters as a quarterback under Alonzo Stagg at Chicago in 1893 and 1894. In 1895 he had coached at Bucknell University, Lewisburg, Pennsylvania. The liberality of eligibility rules in the early years suggests that he might also have played at Bucknell, but if he did, it was under a pseudonym or he failed to make the team he coached. He moved to South Bend with his mother in 1896 to coach, quarterback and captain the football team the first year; he also taught English and studied law. He was partly paid in cuts of beef from the Notre Dame farm, run by the Brothers of Holy Cross. I saw Hering play once—in 1906 as the member of a local professional club at a time when he already had become well known as an after-dinner speaker, a high official of the F.O.E., and editor of the *Eagle* magazine. He had the jaw of a fighting man and the brooding look of a poet; you could read these traits in the 1896 group picture. In later life he brought out a volume of his poetic compositions. He became most widely known as the "father of Mother's Day," a memorial he promoted as a tribute to his own mother.

Other members of the '90 teams whom I'd meet in after years included such local talent as Buck Hanley, Pete Studebaker, Mike Moritz and Walter Muessel. Their academic status remains a mystery I see no reason to probe profoundly. Certainly they were not tramp athletes in the errant sense of the term. Rather, they were community-spirited citizens of South Bend, let's say, who loved to play football and had no prejudice against rubbing elbows with higher education. Only one, a jolly barkeeper when I first knew him, is listed as a monogram winner: Francis X. (Buck) Hanley. Pete was a scion of the wagon- and carriage-making Studebakers, world famed. The Muessels were local brewers of Silver Edge Beer, notable for the dependably good head on it. I became acquainted with Mike Moritz around 1910 when I was a fires reporter and he was a driver or hoseman, indoor baseball and pinochle star at Central Fire Station. His exposure to the academic side of life, or its proximity, hadn't done his fine Irish nature any discernible harm.

The only bona fide bird on the wing at that time I've heard of dropped off long enough to wear out his welcome almost on sight. A Saturday or two later Notre Dame was in Chicago to play the Maroons, and lined up against them was this Wellington. A South Bend newspaper accused A. A. Stagg, alleged paragon and proclaimed apostle of simon purity in college sports, of having rung in a notorious ringer. It baldly questioned the sincerity of Stagg's militant espousal of all-out amateurism.

Stagg defended his use of the tramp on the basis that the game with Notre Dame had been scheduled as a practice scrimmage under game conditions. By his decision, the two schools never met again on the gridiron. Whether the Wellington affair was responsible doesn't appear to have been resolved. The Maroons had had the best of the scoreboard in four confrontations, for practice or for real: 8-0, 18-0, 34-5, 23-5. But they may have got the worst of the bumps. There's some intimation of this in the Chicago *Tribune*'s account of the 1898 meeting, as reprinted in the South Bend *Times*. "Farley and other Notre Dame players," it reported, "were taken out for rough play." Apparently Stagg could afford to let them back on the field in the second half. The score at half time was 22-5, and Chicago made 13 points thereafter. But according to the *Tribune*, as "the moon was chasing shadows on the Marshall Field gridiron" and final time was called, "the score could as easily have been 60-5." This assumption, we can believe, the Notre Dames would have challenged to the last man. They couldn't be beaten in their hearts, and their scoreboard conquerors might pay a bruising price on the field for victory.

In spite of a one-sideness greater than reflected by the score in the *Tribune*'s appraisal, it observes that ". . . the game was the most remarkable of all games in the West on one account." It expounds: ". . . for the first time the Princeton place-kick was successfully made in a regular game [N.B. a "practice" game to Coach Stagg?]. The Maroons have been practicing among themselves on the new kick of the Tigers, but when the men from Hoosierdom made the formation for its trial on the Chicago 30-yard line, the defenders were puzzled. There was a hitch in the Notre Dame signals and the men fell into a position that looked like a preparation for punt, and yet it was not the conventional formation. A whisper of 'fake kick' came from the sidelines; but when Mullin [John Mullen, captain] took the ball and placed it on the ground a thrill of pleased surprise went around and grew into loud applause when Daly kicked the pigskin calmly between the uprights."

The five points awarded for this introductory showing of the place-kick in "Western" game competition was the first blood drawn that day and the last, figuratively taken, for Notre Dame. But the incident illustrated the crowd appeal of the Gold and Blue wearers even in decisive defeat by points. It symbolizes further the intellectual aggressiveness that traditionally has distinguished Notre Dame strategy except for the recent recession from the norm. I've read elsewhere a citation of Notre Dame's pioneering part in acquainting the West with the flying wedge or some such devastating formation in returning kickoffs. It was in this spirit of initiative and experimentation less than a decade later, still before Rockne, that Notre Dame, ahead of all big schools, integrated the still experimental forward pass with the rest of its offense.

Probably the best all-around athlete of the nineteenth century at Notre Dame (football, baseball, track) was John F. Farley, whom I would come to know as Notre Dame's most unforgettable prefect. Traditionalists who remember him in the prime of his prefecture would praise and thank the Lord if Father Farley could revisit the campus long enough to curl a long whip around the tails of panty-raiders and other infiltrators of the Notre Dame scene at various levels, and to match wits with the craftiest rebels. "King" Farley was a monarch of all and everybody he surveyed in the undergraduate domain. He could appear as fierce as a tiger and act with a serpent's cunning. He acted first and explained later if a surprise clap on the back or the unannounced flick of his genial lash didn't carry their own lesson and warning. His knack for subtler tactics implemented his strategy in dealing with dwellers in the Corby Hall basement, or "subway," who had been beating bed check by going and coming at will through an unused tunnel. The experience of Pete Vaughan, varsity football and basketball star, was typical. Pete was congratulating himself one night on another successful re-entry from a "skiving" venture when he noticed that his suit was smeared with the grease with which Father Farley had coated the walls of the tunnel.

An amputation put Father John Farley in a wheelchair in his latter days. One of the sad but cherished recollections of the old breed of Notre Dame men is of the last time they saw the man whose heart was as soft for them as his tongue and hand could be hard on them. He had wheeled his chair to the point of entry and departure in the quadrangle to "see the boys off" for vacation or their first grapple with the world. They in turn signaled good-bye not only to "King" Farley but to his era.

I was still playing football at Notre Dame on the occasion

of the first fall Homecoming, 1920. Among the reunionists were "Red" Salmon and Big John Eggeman, the latter a powerful, buoyant personality who confirmed an old impression of his prowess in football, track and baseball around the turn of the century. I have more, much more to write about Salmon. Another delayed acquaintance was with Angus McDonald, star halfback, quarterback and kicker just as the nineteenth century was fading out. In appearance he could have modeled for Calvert's Man of Distinction. He was one of the most gracious of the old-timers I would run across. I met him in the thirties while heading for Los Angeles on the Southern Pacific to scout the Trojans. He was working for the Southern Pacific—as its president.

Assisting Frank Hering in 1898 was his antithesis in background, build and bearing. As I understand it, James J. McWeeney had been a heavyweight wrestler while in the Chicago Police Department. He was said to have worked on the Notre Dame farm. I can't vouch for the chronology, except to note that he was South Bend's chief of police after the turn of the century. Once in a while he spent some time with the high school football squad. I was present as a bystander at practice one afternoon when he dispensed some rugged psychology for the benefit of ball carriers. "Go into the line with your free fist doubled," he advised. "You won't have to use it. Your opponents will get the message." McWeeney was Notre Dame's head coach in 1899. After him it was Pat O'Dea, famous Wisconsin kicker, in 1900 and 1901—he wasn't even a name to me. Jim Garragher is listed coach in 1902, the year the Grants moved to South Bend. I had never heard of him until he turned up at Notre Dame in the 1930's. Elmer Layden, head coach, who had a proper fondness for figures of the tradition, introduced him as an honored guest at a football banquet. He was a dark, gently smiling man we all liked. He'd been a tackle at the turn of the century especially noted for his slashing tackle-around gains.

By the close of the 1901 season the big name in football was Salmon. He had entered Notre Dame as a classical student in 1900 and had switched the next year to civil engineering, a profession of which he made a distinguished lifelong career. One of the subscribers to my weekly newsletter to Notre Dame football fans (1949-50) was Dr. W. W. Halloran, '03, not a varsity athlete. He wrote me as follows:

"In your letter you speak of Louis J. Salmon (Red). I think I was the first one to tackle him. I was captain of the St. Joe Hall team and asked Red if he ever played football. He said, 'Not much' so we put him on the second team. We kicked off. He got the ball. I hardly touched him. And everyone else was on the ground. He was on the goal line standing up. The next day he was playing fullback for the varsity."

That was Red Salmon. To touch him in a campus scrimmage was the equivalent of grounding anybody else! Dan O'Connor, who played varsity baseball with Salmon, confirmed Dr. Halloran's memoir. Dan was one of the St. Joe players he had left sprawling or anchored. It was typical, Dan O'Connor told me, that Red would have thought he wasn't good enough to make the varsity. Actually, according to newspaper records, he played at end most of the first year. Perhaps his modesty accounted for the repeated misspelling of his name. The South Bend newspapers and the student periodical persistently identified him as one "Sammon"—suggesting no attempt on his part to seek a correction; assuming, with some doubt, that he read about himself in the first place.

When Indiana invaded Cartier Field November 16, 1901, the state title was at stake. Purdue already had been beaten, 12-6. Many years would elapse before Notre Dame students would submit to organized cheering as a matter of routine. The undergrad attitude in 1901 was underlined in the South Bend *Tribune* the week of the title game by a report that special "rooter preparations are on a strong scale. Every student will be there whether he likes it or not and take part in organized cheering." Prizes were offered for the best yells composed for the occasion. First prize went to Dominic O'Malley (football, 1899), a native Irish member of the religious community, for a lyric in Gaelic, herewith transcribed from the *Tribune* with no guarantee of fidelity to the original version:

Aurd-skuel aur Mahur
Na laochra town gon go
Feer laoch na mille trown
Skappig eud mor cho
Buallig agus Kawnig eud
Gus kurrig eud fay chra
Aurd-skuel aur Mahur
Go-brach, go-brach.

"This yell," continued the *Tribune*, "is supposed to be sung to the tune of *Marching through Georgia*, but in reality it is a most doleful, bloodcurdling howl, and should have a most demoralizing effect on the football men of Indiana."

Apparently the originality and fearsomeness of "this yell" was not given as much credit for an 18-5 Irish victory as Notre Dame's reputed superiority in straight football and physical condition. There is no record that it ever was heard again on Cartier Field.

The first twelve years of sustained intercollegiate football at Notre Dame almost coincided with the presidency of Father Thomas Walsh's successor, Father Andrew Morrisey. Like Father Walsh, he personally shunned exercise in its various forms. At the same time he rejected the point of view that the work of the university was the development of the mind alone. "The education of the head at the expense of the heart is one of the crying evils of the day," he said, and added, "Athletics . . . to be sure is subordinate to morals and the attainments of the mind, but its functions are positive." He implemented this philosophy by promoting the erection of a large gymnasium (1899) and a larger, finer one in 1901 when the first was destroyed by fire.

My father managed the famous Greenstockings, "independent baseball champions of the West," in 1899 and 1900. He remained in South Bend to clerk in the Sheridan Hotel. He sent for us, my mother, sister and me, at the end of school in June, 1902. I had no notion of it, of course, but my coincidental affinity with Notre Dame, of which I wasn't even aware for many years, acquired a metaphysical complement in reality before I saw the Golden Dome. It happened when my ear was first struck by "the deep and mellow burdon" of the great bell in the tower of the campus chapel, the Church of the Sacred Heart of Jesus. To the students then of Notre Dame, I've read recently, that sound signaled "Solemn High Mass and great ceremony, or fricasseed chicken and square apple pie such as only the Sisters could make." For me downtown, through grade school and high school, the Notre Dame bell had wordless connotations as its booming voice swept over field, meadow, river, valley, tree and roof to wherever we lived in South Bend. Baptized a Roman Catholic, I'd been raised churchless for reasons not pertinent here. I remember best the steel etchings in my mother's King James Bible, the colored illustrations in my book of Bible stories for children, the "Now I Lay Me Down To Sleep" taught me by my mother and recited as a matter of habit: also a petition to the Sacred Heart of Jesus which I repeated after my Catholic paternal grandmother out of grandfilial respect. It would take me almost a lifetime to evolve a conceptual appreciation of the divine authority in the universe on which to pose the faith in which eventually I would be confirmed.

Yet I know now that the voice of the great bell enveloped me in a mood fraught with intimations of immortality. It tolled in my soul the warning of a time of reckoning; it made me feel as I often did alone in the hush of twilight, during the long moment of truth between day and night, when I would be wrapped in a sort of mild ecstasy of mingled fear and hope having to do with something I couldn't define. This something was similar to the feeling that tugged at me whenever I paused before the print on the sitting-room wall of Millet's *Sowers* (I think it was) at the evening Angelus—whatever that was, it would take me half a century to become intellectually curious enough to find out. On the other hand, still so very young, I was too remote from a state of grace ever to catch the rustle of an angel's wings in my reveries, an illusion vouchsafed me more than once when I was much older and wickeder, still wandering, with less excuse, in a waste world of involuntary apostasy. Had I known that Notre Dame was French for Our Lady, I still would not have understood the significance of her statue on the Dome, for the reason that I wouldn't have cared. When I was ten, for me the symbol of Notre Dame the institution was not the Golden Dome or the golden figure of the Mother of God surmounting it. It was a living personality, a redheaded fullback. My image of Red Salmon as a Notre Dame man is my bond with the school, not my years at Notre Dame on the field and in the classroom. It is the Notre Dame that Red Salmon represented, and still represents in my memory, for which I carry an affection transcending an old man's discomfort in the face of change.

7

I don't think I saw Red Salmon play. Yet I have in the file of memory a concept of the great redhead in action. It must be a composite of what I'd read and heard of him with his likeness seen on a black and white window poster prominently displayed around town. I'm looking at a copy now. It shows him wearing a laced canvas jacket, canvas or moleskin pants with corrugated padding, shin guards and high laced boots. He is posed to punt. His unhelmeted head is protected by a heavy mane of wavy hair—right, it's red, perhaps auburn. His features remind me of Kirk Douglas as seen in motion pictures in his twenties.

Father Cornelius Hagerty, my instructor at Notre Dame in ontology, as a student sat next to Salmon in class. His cheeks were so smooth, the color so solid, that his skin appeared translucent, according to Father Hagerty. The blue of his eyes was "startling." Quiet, reserved, he was what an opponent described as "a red-headed, blue-eyed, apple-cheeked so-and-so on the football field."

He wasn't the 'huge crashing type of fullback" described in *A Treasury of Notre Dame Football*. He couldn't be even loosely depicted as "the Nagurski of his time," the way one historian recalled him. Bronko Nagurski was hefty enough to have played tackle at Minnesota, usually overrun by giant candidates for the line, before being shifted to fullback and going on to his greatest renown in professional football.

Salmon indeed blasted the line with the impact of a heavyweight, but he stood less than five-ten and weighed between 165 and 170 pounds. He was shiftier, more versatile than the immortal Bronk. Born a little later, he would have been an ideal triple threat.

Salmon punted, kicked off, and drop-kicked from the field and for points-after. He was a breakaway potential on kickoff and punt returns. He was a first-rate blocker. He was reputed to be the only linebacker able to stop the great Willie Heston of Michigan consistently even as the Wolverines dominated the scoreboard. A Western press association circulated his halftone with the caption of "Greatest Back in the West." At a time when it was a red-letter event for a Western Conference or a Michigan star to breach the ivy walls of Walter Camp's All-America lineup, Red Salmon of tiny Notre Dame made the third team.

Some years ago, as already noted, at the climax of Frank Leahy's coaching regime at Notre Dame, I published a series of weekly letters for Notre Dame football followers which were introduced with an issue in which I nominated Red Salmon for my all-time Notre Dame team and backed my choice with contemporary newspaper testimony of his prowess, such as: ". . . Salmon, the mainstay of his team . . . tore the Purple line as if made of wet paper." . . . "When Salmon was forced to punt, the ball went 65 yards." . . . or "he sent the ball spiraling 75 yards." . . . (These were mostly remarks culled from Chicago sports pages; one reporter insisted that he could curve his punts right or left at will.) "Salmon . . . he who never fails to gain. . . ." "When not crashing . . . line or skirting . . . ends . . . he was in the interference pulling a companion to the front . . . on defensive also a star."

I talked later to Harley Kirby, a great trackman at Notre Dame who played football with Salmon in 1902. Harley was playing professional football in Ohio when Red was graduated from Notre Dame. Going to work immediately on a major engineering project in New York, Red spent his first two weeks' vacation with the Massillon Club, his only venture into professional football. The pros had been more impressed by their grapevine report on him than by Walter Camp's gesture. He was a players' player. For three games, Harley said, Salmon received $1,500, a fabulous sum when a dollar was a dollar and eggs were ten cents a dozen. Salmon was impressed, he would tell me, by the professional know-how, but was not to be diverted from his original commitment to an engineering career as a full-time involvement.

A number of years ago Harley Kirby settled in South Bend to live out his retirement with a sister. Not long before his death in 1959 we discussed Salmon. Harley had done some coaching, he'd followed Notre Dame closely and critically for more than half a century; he had seen all our great fullbacks in action since Salmon. He still ranked the redhead as the greatest. Salmon could have breached a literal brick wall, Harley soberly assured me. I felt that this tribute was magnified, at least validated rather than diminished by the realism of his parenthetical postscript: "Of course, if the wall did stand firm by a remote chance, a couple of us were always on hand, prepared to lift him by the belt and throw him over the top."

In 1903, both captained and coached by Louis J. "Red"

Salmon, Notre Dame was unbeaten and unscored on in nine games and was tied once. The 0-0 standoff was with Northwestern's Wildcats, who had played Wisconsin and Chicago even and had defeated Illinois. The Notre Dames thought they had won and would have rejoiced in an immediate rematch with traditional confidence. This was indeed an old Notre Dame custom. As early as 1896 they had grasped for at least a handle on the Western championship despite having lost three games before they met Beloit in the season's last test. Beloit had tied Northwestern 6-6 and had given way to Wisconsin by only 6-0. Since Northwestern and Wisconsin were the best Western teams of popular record in 1896, Notre Dame had claimed the title by the margin of a two-point comparative superiority based on the Gold and Blue setback of Beloit by 8-0!

The 1903 contention had more intrinsic merit. For one thing, when a young man of Captain-Coach Salmon's intelligence, integrity and habitual reticence made a public statement that Notre Dame should have had a perfect season—undefeated, unscored on *and* untied—I for one, now as then, cannot question either his sincerity or his judgment.

A follow-up criterion of the class of the 1903 team was the game with Wabash. The Crimson had beaten Indiana, had held a representative Purdue to a score of 17-0, and had just missed copping the secondary college championship of Indiana by an upset. Salmon and friends disposed of this customer, an intermittent pest to Notre Dame football teams, to the tune of 35-0. Except for the Michigan Aggies, the rest of the schedule was short of modern name value, but the season's total of 292 points to 0, against opponents whose least enrollment was comparable with Notre Dame's eligible student power, would have been worthy of respect in any ranking, notwithstanding that it did not put us into acknowledged championship consideration outside Indiana.

Salmon's most dramatic performance was a one-man march in a losing effort against Michigan in 1902. The game was played in the rain at Toledo, Ohio. Oddly, the score by which Michigan won, 23-0, would rank Notre Dame with the best of the rest of the West on the basis of comparative scores.

The Wolverines, not then in the Western Conference, hadn't been beaten since 1900. They were on a fantastic winning binge, interrupted only once—by a 6-6 tie with Minnesota. This epic victory march would last until the last game of 1905, when Chicago nosed in on a safety, 2-0—a battle of the giants which I, then a Walter Eckersall fan, read all about in the Chicago *American*.

During that fabulous five years, the Wolverines' opponents scored in 56 games a combined total of 38 points! Their own scoring would have challenged a computer; the grand sum is suggested by the 372 points to 0 amassed against just four teams in 1902: Indiana, Michigan Aggies, Ohio State and Iowa. Of this group Indiana made the best showing—holding Hurry-up Yost's mighty minions to a score of 60-0. Two leaders in the Western Conference, Chicago and Minnesota, succumbed respectively 21-0 and 23-6. As the Notre Dame game went in 1902, the Gold and Blue were only one step short of scoring a touchdown that would have reduced Michigan's margin to 17 points and have given Notre Dame a tie with Minnesota in a comparison of scores.

Red Salmon had been unstoppable play after play from past the middle of the field and appeared on the verge of crossing the goal line when he slipped in the mud on the last down of the vital series. This was the anticlimax to a one-man classic over which Notre Dame men would revel in the recountal for years. For at least a generation it was challenged in our football lore only by the story of how Pete Vaughan broke the goal post when Notre Dame finally tamed the Wolverines in 1909.

Salmon's legendary drive in 1902 began on his 48-yard line, 57 yards from a touchdown. Legend sets us back against our own goal at the start. But on a soggy field, against an apparently superior team, the fact was not far behind the myth, although Salmon did not carry the ball quite eleven straight times, as popularly recounted. The sequence was broken once after he had advanced nine yards to Michigan's 52-yard line "in two smashes." At that point a worthy back named Frank Lonergan, future West Coast judge, rounded end to the Michigan 44. But from there it was all Salmon on eight straight bucks, averaging almost 5½ yards (without benefit of a forward passing threat), only to miss the TD by a literal slip between figurative cup and lip.

Those who knew Red Salmon and admired the way he played football did so with a warm regard for his character and personality that seem to communicate a counterpart of appreciation to persons who had never met him or even had not seen him perform. Of all his worshipful fans in his heyday, I could have been the most; certainly I wasn't the least. When I came to know him a bit personally, I understood why this particular image of boyhood hero worship, appearing to me before I became conscious of a type that would be identified as "a Notre Dame man," had never faded.

Salmon was persuaded only twice to return to the campus. I think his reluctance stemmed from sincere diffidence, true humility. The first time was in 1920. I was still playing, after a long time-out in service. Next to the extraordinary George

Gipp, who ran just once that Homecoming Day (if memory serves me), for 70 yards and a touchdown, Red Salmon, '05, was the Homecoming hero. The students loved him. They held him over the weekend and gave him a mass send-off on the train east he finally made. I was coaching when he returned the second time, in the 1930's, and head coach Elmer Layden, deferring to my identification in time with the old days, appointed me as a one-man welcoming committee and special guide. This rare privilege I selfishly engrossed at every opportunity, in company with Dan O'Connor. At the time I maintained a bachelors' roost in which my chief companion and head chef was my Uncle Angus. He was managing the South Bend Greenstockings when Red and Dan played varsity ball. After a long evening, the convivial particulars of which I don't recall, we repaired to 221 Tonti (named for La Salle's lieutenant, Henry Tonti) at 4:00 A.M., and Uncle Angus, a short-order cook between seasons when he was very young, came up with ham and eggs. Dan and I carried the burden of dialogue. In retrospect I find something archangelic in Red Salmon's faintly smiling reticence, as if he had come incognito from afar, bearing understanding and empathy for frailties which his own superior nature transcended without pride.

(My uncle's quiet enjoyment of the occasion had something of the same implication. A professional athlete in his time, a man in love with life and people, Angus Grant was at home in any company, a good listener who could be forceful and fluent enough in his turn.)

Salmon the engineer was accustomed to dealing with projects, situations and men on the grand scale, yet you felt that he had profound respect for the smallest things that engaged others. It was good to be with him. I knew now why the students had been so taken with him back in 1920. Perhaps while with him you were hoping to break through to the deep-down-inside Salmon because you felt that would be an even more rewarding experience. At the same time you knew that you didn't rate that favor and it was all right.

The men who knew Salmon best were his greatest admirers. Bill Draper from Chicago was one of these. A great athlete in his own right, Bill won his first football monogram in 1904, but he captained the track team when Salmon was still competing. Several years ago we were discussing the great redhead. The last time they'd been together in New York, Salmon had intimated some question of the course his life had taken. I was surprised when Draper recalled that Red Salmon had come to Notre Dame from an Eastern seminary. If he had his life to do over—this was Bill Draper's deduction—he wondered whether he wouldn't pursue his original inclination toward a religious vocation. This deep vein of spirituality helped explain his impact on his fellows of any age. If a buried doubt increased his natural reserve, no vain regret had soured him in the process. This Red Salmon, our first football legend, surely was the complete layman the Founders of Notre Dame dedicated themselves to turn out.

8

The drive to play rough games is congenitally implanted too profoundly in certain boys to be grubbed out by persuasion, legislation or decree. Somebody should be thankful that such boys today are able to begin playing football under competent adult organization, instruction and supervision. But the principle of participation was the same on the old-fashioned corner lot. We might start out with pom-pom-pull-away (we called it Blackman, I think), which is a tag game, but before long we'd be tackling. Nor did we need a ball to get the ball rolling in something more like football. A bundle of rags would do and our cross-tag and Blackman background would suggest a run-and-tackle game.

Assuming we had an inflated bag to begin with, we might kick it for a while. But in either case intragroup contact would evolve. Let enough kids show up for a team, you looked around for outside competition. Let the other group prove superior, you tried to recruit better players, to practice more and harder, and, if necessary and practicable, enlist somebody older, and pertinently experienced, to teach fundamentals and tactics. And there's always somebody to watch somebody else do something besides watch. That's the innocuous root of the "Big Gate Evil"!

The better both sides played, the more interesting the game to them and to the sprinkling of sideliners attracted by a rugged spectacle. With or without a crowd, with or without a coach, both sides were out to win in accordance with rules that defined the conduct and rewards of the game, including provision for fair enforcement that automatically created a demand for a formal or informal arbiter.

The aspirants who didn't qualify for the active lineup practiced until they were acceptable, or turned to another group closer to their own talent level. If a kid quit, except for physical disability or some overpowering conflict of interests, such as parental objection, it was because football turned out not to be his dish. Occasionally, a boy might sample the game with reservations and discover or develop an appetite for rough recreation. Without an inherent love for the rough stuff, he wouldn't make the hamburger squad in school.

Brute force is, always has been, ever will be an integral element of football; it's a natural by-product of the binatured human condition. But football is far from being as brutal or brutalizing as magazine headlines like this one would move us to believe: "FOOTBALL IS GOING BERSERK. A game ruled by force needs a housecleaning." This professional debunker is crying over a never-never kind of football, implying that once-upon-a-lovely-time-had-by-all it had been only a vigorous version of ring-around-the-rosy or face tag. Today's footballers come much bigger; but not any tougher, let's say. For instance, that resounding impact you hear today often records collision between two sets of gridiron armor which in the ruder days we didn't possess. In any case, if football today (the college brand is meant) needs a housecleaning, it isn't because force has pre-empted unduly the functions of human reason and will. On the contrary, the game is more complex, more demanding upon intellect and imagination than ever.

We were living in a flat less than a block from the cottage that housed us on first arrival in South Bend. Hence, I must have been between twelve and thirteen when I bruised my knee. At the time three or four kids in the neighborhood were meeting afternoons and Saturdays on a corner common not far from the flat, each taking a turn trying to run through the others with a rag ball. My knee shook like jelly when I walked. This condition helped develop my speed. I preferred to dodge, but I owed it to my ailing joint to run away from contact as fast as I could. It never occurred to me to give up this game until my knee returned to normal. My father worked seven to seven, seven days a week; we seldom saw each other at home and I stayed away from the hotel during this period. That's the way the kids were—I think a lot of them still are: a basic reason for supervised football at an early age. When Uncle Angus came visiting, he hustled me into the bathroom and wouldn't let me go until we had got rid of the swelling. It took hours of hot-water treatment.

We visited my grandparents in Defiance every vacation. One of my intimates there was one of the finest young athletes I've ever encountered. Besides being swift afoot, Riley Wortman threw and batted right- and left-handed with equal skill. He was clever with the gloves; he was an adept wrestler. If he'd played basketball he would have been a great shot. He swam like a fish; I'm pretty sure he skated the Maumee River from the mouth of Bean Creek to the five-mile dam. He could handle any kind of river craft. I admired especially the deftness with which he handled his first set of feathered sculls. The first time he kicked a football he achieved a long, high spiral and that would be his routine form. He would have been a great triple-threat artist but for one thing—he didn't care enough for the game to endure hard physical contact, or to court it for the purpose of evading it.

His antithesis was my favorite football player when I was still a closet gridder myself. This was the fictional figure of mighty mites of factual college football like Charlie Daly of Harvard and the smallest of the Poes, who often fulfilled the demands of their assignments far beyond any precalculated letter, offensing and defensing with an abandon that soared above the element of brutality in physical impact. "Shorty Wilson" will have to do for the forgotten name of my hero. I found him more appealing than *Frank Merriwell at Yale* at five cents a copy. Shorty Wilson's adversaries, far weightier on the average, battered his flesh, rattled his bones, black-and-blued him some days from ankle to hairline—not to discharge any submerged hostilities toward his person, or life in general, but to neutralize if possible this key performer's capacity for frustrating their legitimate intention to win the ball game.

All herein concerned simply accepted the fact and hazard of bumps and bruises and occasional breaks as the necessary contingent of the execution of their assigned parts, of which physical contact was a hard condition. Nor did Shorty Wilson submit to unavoidable harsh, grueling physical punishment in order to demonstrate his sportsmanship or build his character. He conformed with the specifications of sportsmanship to forestall penalty or possible expulsion from the game a violation of a rule might incur. Whether his character was being built was vitally related to the principles and conditions under which the game was sponsored, coached, promoted and played.

Character building, precious potentiality, is an incidental and uninsured value. Face it. To expose a boy to fracture and concussion, possibly fatal injury, primarily to mold his character is stupid; it can be reprehensible. We always come back to the basic justification—that something Riley Wortman didn't have for football—love. Love for what this game is:

rock-and-sock athletic competition. College football is for rock-and-sock kids grown up. Coaches and recruiters generally recognize this circumstance. But often they cater to parental misunderstanding of the need as well as the urge of some young males for rugged physical expression by allowing, if not encouraging, the misconstruction of the potential of character building as a guarantee. Equally unacceptable is a male parent's prideful itch to perpetuate his own athletic name, or a frustrated duffer's drive to compensate through his son, or an obsession for vicarious familial participation.

Shorty Wilson figurates the *raison d'être* of football because his primary commitment was to the fulfillment of his own nature and desire: the self-willed satisfaction of his particular compulsion to play this game to the ultimate of the schooled and disciplined powers, the trained talent and controlled ardor of an artist-athlete.

Granted the character-building latency of football, this was the way for Shorty to capitalize; that is, by doing what he wanted to do with everything he had. What he gave to the game of his potential best, it gave back of its best potential. At worst, it seems safe to concede that playing football is better for the player's better self (I don't have to argue that point, do I?) than forward-passing Molotov cocktails for sport or even for an unauthorized cause; or setting fire to cats or cutting tires. As a safety valve for the animal spirits of the gladiatorial complex, football's service to one and all seems worth weighing. Specifically, more positively, football played for love can be especially good for that human quality which the Latins in this instance have the word for: *fortitudo.*

Football, along with kindred sports incurring severe physical risks and a variety of mental and spiritual challenges and pressures, provides an exceptional course in fortitude. The properly coached youth is conditioned to overcome natural aversions to diverse stresses, and at the same time to discipline any emotional tendency to overcommit himself unreasonably. He learns to conquer intelligent fear and control instinctive daring—a fortuitous habit of mind and will that plainly can be extended and applied to other areas of human stress and strain.

As a rough-and-ready friend of mine once said of good manners, which he admired, I also must say of proper coaching when I was a kid: I only wish I'd had some myself. This is the kind of accredited Spartan training I had not had when I was around thirteen and tried to tackle a visiting kid of about my size from Chicago with a ball or a substitute under his arm. When he straight-armed me in the throat with his fist and then convinced me that it was a legal act of self-defense, I was through even playing *at* football. The short memory and resilience of youth, of course, soon dissipated that perhaps sensible resolution.

In the winter of 1906 I saw Captain Bill Draper of the Notre Dame track team taking the hurdles during the indoor season. I'd entered high school at midyear, just before turning fourteen. A little later I was on hand to watch my uncle's Central Leaguers training in the dirt-floored Big Gym. It thrilled me to see an infield workout indoors. When they moved outside I saw the Greenstockings and the Notre Dame varsity nine in a practice game. Among the Gold and Blue diamond stars then was John A. Dubuc, also a varsity basketballer the following year, destined to pitch for the Detroit Tigers, as he followed and preceded many other Notre Damers who enjoyed more than a cup of java in the Big Show. That fall I rooted for Notre Dame's recently graduated Draper and Bill Silver, along with Frank Hering, in the lineup of the South Bend Athletic Association vs. the Physicians and Surgeons of Chicago, on the Central League baseball grounds at Springbrook Park.

In that wonderful year of 1906 when Harry (Red) Miller, eldest of the famous football brothers from my native Defiance, entered Notre Dame and the forward pass was legalized, I made the high school's baseball second team and played my first formal game of football, also with the high school seconds.

By express or tacit parental edict, I forget which, football was still banned from my life, and I resisted Maurice Myers' repeated attempts to line me up for a game, except once. Maurice was captain of the baseball as well as the football seconds. He had never seen me even play at football, but I had enlisted his full confidence in my athletic capacity by my self-drilled capacity for chasing a deep fly ball in the outfield with my back to the home plate and turning at the witching moment to make the catch look easy.

The football game I finally consented to take part in was scheduled for Springbrook Park. I'd just got into long pants —a discarded pair of my father's. At fourteen I'd just about attained his arrested height of five feet six inches (leaving me only an inch to grow). Captain-Coach Myers provided a pair of moleskins, but there was no secure spot to check my new-old long pants; so I pulled them up to my knees and pulled the moleskins over. I think Maurice had some other equipment for me—probably a head guard, possibly nose and shin guards; no cleated shoes, I'm sure. The worn red turtleneck sweater I'd play in, a castoff of my uncle's, was the one I'd left home in. What price shining armor! The action would be the thing.

Shortly before game time our key man, a ringer, hadn't

shown up. He lived across the river in River Park. Maurice delegated a stalwart soul named Sherwood Tucker to round up this badly needed missing person. They thought two heads might be more persuasive than one in case our man was reluctant as well as tardy. I would have preferred to refuse my head. The bridge at this point was undergoing repairs and the only way across was on a three-plank walk for the workmen that to me appeared like a weaving ribbon that would challenge a tightwire pedestrian. Heights froze me, but, of course, I couldn't admit it. I still marvel that I made that crossing without plunging some twenty-five feet or so into the St. Joseph River. But I do have a theory, based on the subsequent discovery that heights in an airplane do not induce the sensation of wanting to take off on my own. It seems that it is only when I stand high up on a rigid surface with no handhold that I experience the fear of falling and the dread that I might jump. From all this comes the conditional assumption that the give and sway of that plank walk saved me. I remember hoping that if I lost my balance it would be at a point where the water was reasonably deep.

It was a purely psychological factor that made the return crossing a breeze. Our star had to be told the signals and I elected to be the communicator. In retrospect I can't explain how I knew them well enough myself to undertake their transmission. Obviously, the distraction eased my tension. Indeed, I didn't suffer a fleeting qualm of apprehension. The long way over was the short way back.

I've no idea how the game unfolded. It seems to me I made tackle after tackle from right end, because nobody did anything to interfere with me when I rushed across the line. But that developed after the first play, an end sweep on my side. I knew what to do. Take a couple of steps across the line of scrimmage and tackle this lone stranger. The head was willing, but the feet wouldn't mind. I didn't know it at the time but experience was offering me a lesson on the spot. I was the victim of a physical inertia, the penalty for waiting flat-footed for the runner to show his intention to go inside or outside. If my feet had been in slight motion in place, preliminary to the maneuver of commitment, I would have been relaxed enough to react sharply. I didn't catch on. It took frustration and chagrin to egg me into the opposite extreme on the next play. At the snap of the ball I charged at an acute angle and it just happened nobody seemed to care. The tailback was a set-up duck. He didn't seem to expect me. Or maybe he was a flat-footed thinker, too. A blocker could have sideswiped me into an adjoining county. But nobody seemed to be around except the duck and me. I banged into him with my shoulder and down we tumbled.

It was a new feeling. Something had been added to the fun of throwing an opponent hard in a wrestling match. You were involved in something outside yourself, bigger than you. You hadn't been sure you could fit into this foreign pattern. As an individual achievement it was eminently satisfactory. But here you had achieved within the framework of something beyond and above your individual concern and commitment. There was a new, special satisfaction in having done this thing in conformance with a pattern of conditions outside your power to establish or control individually. Yes, it was a grand feeling you had without having an inkling of the contextual reasons why.

The thrill of contributing to a competitive cause in athletics involving the group to me was not new—hadn't I experienced it that spring playing baseball for my admired friend, Maurice Myers? But I did know that it was not the same kind of kick

I'd got out of this football game. What I didn't recognize was the occasion of this difference in my pleasure, the fact that in football the identification with your teammates is more critical than in baseball. On offense, for example, the team effort of the players involves more interdependence among members in every new situation and consequently must be more unified to work. Another basic distinction is football's stronger appeal to the more primitive emotions because of the more primitive nature of play-by-play issues and their resolution.

I would see Paul Hornung make more tackles for old Notre Dame in a single Saturday afternoon than I would make in three seasons. But if I'd never made another tackle after the first one, I'd remember the rugged fun it was to play football when young and jumping with ginger, and afraid to be afraid.

9

In my teens, during the first decade of this century, I became a demifamiliar of that area of the Notre Dame scene where the athletic action was. Until I was fourteen or so, however, I was more likely to read about the Notre Dame athletes than watch them perform. Beginning in 1906 I began to take in the varsity events that didn't conflict with my own athletic involvements, some of which took me on campus. I played basketball at least once in the Carroll Hall gym, with the high school seconds, and with the same group against this or another hall team wall to wall in the Big Gym, where I also took part in a high school interclass meet. Twice we played Corby Hall (1908 and 1909) in baseball, splitting even. We never left the campus without the refreshment of lemonade and Number Fours (chocolate-coated vanilla cookies with a nut on top) in Brother "Leep's" little store behind "Spit" Hall next to the Big Gym, if we had a nickel or a dime. Many years later it would surprise me to learn that tiny Brother Leopold was a violinist who had taught in the School of Music.

How did that cheer go? "He's a man. Who's a man? JOHN DOE. Rah, rah, rah. He's a Notre Dame man." Maybe the students still yell it—or a parody thereof! I don't attend pep rallies and at the games I apparently don't pay attention, or I'm not seated where I can make out the words. It's possible the whole ritual is in the football program; if so it's one section I pass over lightly, perhaps because my image of the Notre Dame man formed without benefit of organized cheering. He seems to have eased into my estimation as a special if not superperson.

The young men who came to Notre Dame—from near and, mostly, far—normally arrived with a preconception implanted by heritage or repute, enriched and cultivated by imagination and sentiment. This process preceded the emergence into intercollegiate athletic competition late in the eighties. The geographical spread of the school's appeal to athletically inclined students is plainly patterned by the first football roster (1887), composed of youths who were on campus before a single varsity sport had been established. The pioneer gridders, fourteen of them—Cartier, Cusack, Fehr, Houck, Hepburn, Jewett, Luhn, Maloney, Melady, Nelson, O'Regan, Prudhomme, Sawkins, Springer—came from thirteen states respectively as follows: Michigan, Nebraska, Kentucky, Oregon, Texas, Illinois, Washington, Missouri, Minnesota (Melady), Iowa, Minnesota (O'Regan), Louisiana, Ohio and Georgia.

Once on the site, they might encounter practical disillusionments and frustrations, nevertheless they were spiritually and emotionally clutched forever by that uniqueness that representative sports, especially football, would progressively dramatize.

If Notre Dame harbored any athletes who came to college primarily to play baseball or football, one inducement before 1913 was the chance to see action with a first-rate team without a long year of qualifying residence. This could be a legitimate lure to an athlete who also planned to hit the books. In either case, a student of varsity caliber could count on a ride or a job. I've noted that the stars stayed on year after year. At worst they had the benefit of the education to be salvaged from elbow-rubbing with students and teachers gathered from many walks of life, from all corners of the nation and from beyond. It's understandable that this educative process is not only disreputable today, but impractical. Computers don't have elbows. Let's hope they do someday.

Traditionally the Notre Dame scheme of education began with the first game. The Minims of the elementary school loved the varsity athletes, the Preps admired and emulated them. The university students, especially but not exclusively the athletes, rough and ready in some ways, were cast by the system in the role of Big Brothers, although they would have disowned the term. The tradition was molded, hardened and stamped in this environment of personal responsibility to a younger generation, and it persisted, even after the schools had been discontinued, the Preps first and the Minims in the late 1920's.

Poise and maturity seemed to be the mark of the traditional Notre Dame athlete. The strict disciplines of community control and direction served to challenge and sharpen personal initiative, rather than stifle or thwart it. In varsity competition, the teamwork was achieved without shackling individuality.

When I was fifteen a carnival was pitched on the common near where I lived, in September. I'd made the high school baseball team that spring and had been elected captain. Never mind that there'd been only two other candidates from the 1907 squad, I thought pretty well of myself about that time. But, O, how I envied the slender youth in the carnival crowd with the pleasing tenor voice. No matter that he had not at all the appearance of a varsity athlete, or even an interhall tiger. One of the tent shows featured a sweet songstress with whom I conventionally fell in love, from an infinite distance, not only because she was pretty, but because, of course, she was years older. When she invited the audience to join in the chorus of *Are You Sincere?* the young man in the front row led the response. Nobody around South Bend but a Notre Dame student, athlete or not, arriving early for the opening of school, could have carried off this impromptu role with comparable poise and charm. Of this at least one South Bend High Schooler was absolutely and painfully certain.

As the foregoing episode illustrates, we didn't regard that certain bearing, that *qu'est ce que*, that *que voulez-vous* later to become identified as the hallmark of the athletic Notre Dame spirit, as the exclusive property of athletes. We assumed the Notre Dame spirit was contagious, infecting each and every Notre Dame man by association. The downtowner could recognize the Notre Dame student at a glance, any age. Even the older Prep had a distinctive air or aura that set him apart from the townie. It reflected the zestful belligerence we assign to the Gael, in union with the also spirited *savoir-faire* of the Gaul, both impregnated with a diversity of other national characteristics to spice the composite. Call it individual verve, situation nonchalance, *esprit de corps*. Whatever it was, in moments of crisis, including those in athletic competition, he performed with a sort of trained and disciplined fury for which the French have the precise term, *sangfroid*—literally cold blood, connoting the capacity to act aggressively and coolly under pressure. He was a rugged rooter; individually or in spontaneous unison with fellow rooters (a co-operative action into which he could not be coerced or cajoled normally), he could blast the welkin on occasion from the depths of his being without giving way to the veritable hysteria that sometimes seizes our more cultured modern assemblies.

We didn't put these reactions to words then, of course (luckily?), but we felt them, and they were justified at least to the extent that we experienced such a feeling; and it persisted in my case, after I went to work and Knute Rockne came to Notre Dame, during the first five years out of high school as I played Sunday baseball, week-night basketball, once-or-twice-a-year football (alumni vs. high school); besides squeezing in a couple seasons of organized bush baseball incognito. Notre Dame varsity athletes were no longer heroes on a pedestal to me then. But as fellow athletes of my own age bracket they still borrowed that extra special oomph or value from being at Notre Dame, and we could appreciate it without envy or shallow imitation.

I was a more fervid booster of Notre Dame during my downtown schooldays than ever again. After high school my partisanship, however, was no less genuine or positive. I became simply more objective, a perspective not essentially altered by playing and coaching relations with the Gold and Blue. Certainly at no time have I confused myself with the Notre Dame man of my teens, and that Notre Dame man might hardly recognize himself in the portrayal of his impact on my youth. But there had to be something true and solid in the prototype to fix such a lasting image in my mind and commit me to a profile of rugged romanticism which may seem to abuse the literary license of hyperbole.

About 10 per cent of Notre Dame's current enrollment, I see by the South Bend *Tribune*, quoting the Notre Dame *Scholastic*, is represented by a type the *Tribune* identifies as the "*new* student." They are disciples or creatures of what Alumni Secretary Jim Armstrong labeled the "*now* taste" of some students and faculty members, the desire to mix in with the problems of society. To this "new" or "now" student, my Notre Dame man of the early twentieth century would be an absurd anachronism if he ever existed, to be lumped with the hulking bulk of his fellow undergrads today, whom the "now man" rejects from his class as "carbon copies," "stereotypes," "conformists" who like football, beer and their identification with a Notre Dame to which they came for the primary purpose of getting an education, of all things. The "now student" distinguishes himself from the mob as a "committed" and "articulate" being whose big reason for being at the moment is commitment to a game articulated as "identity crisis."

The "now student" at Notre Dame belongs to a small minority. But he is the articulate one, he is the big noise, and as Jim Armstrong points out, his commitment against orthodoxy may be "not only valid but valuable." He can't, he shouldn't be reciprocally rejected out of hand by us conformists. But to stand for Notre Dame's dedicated educational purpose, to realize it more fully, I'd still take *my* Notre Dame man if he was only half the man I took him to be when baseball was Notre Dame's major varsity sport. For instance, I'll take Mike Powers, Notre Dame's baseball man.

By the time Knute Rockne showed up at Notre Dame the Gold and Blue baseball teams had won 145 games while losing 40 in more formidable competition than early football teams encountered overall. The schedule included the leading teams of the Western Conference, some year after year. The spring preceding Rockne's advent Notre Dame had won all of 21 games but three—and these were home-and-home splits with Arkansas, Michigan Aggies and Michigan. In 1909 they had won all of their 21 games but one, a defeat by Vermont on an Eastern trip during which they met and overcame Syracuse, Williams, Dartmouth, Boston, Fordham, and Georgetown. Among the future major-league stars of this period I recall having seen in an intercollegiate game or a practice game with South Bend's Central Leaguers were Ed Reulbach, John Dubuc, Bert Daniels, George Cutshaw and Fred "Cy" Williams. Phil "Peaches" O'Neill and Bobby Lynch were a bit before my time in South Bend, although I would meet Bobby during World War I when he was K. of C. club director at Camp Shelby, Mississippi. Antedating all these was Mike Powers, varsity catcher in 1897 and 1898, when my Uncle Angus Grant was playing downtown with the Greenstockings. He returned for the commencement exercises of 1908 to play with the alumni in the only game the Gold and Blue varsity lost that spring.

Mike Powers died the year before Knute Rockne came along. This was an athlete whose life reflected as much honor on the Notre Dame idea as would Rockne's although it was less dramatic and was accorded considerably less national notice by volume. On April 26, 1909, we read in the 1909 *Dome*, the senior yearbook, there "died in Philadelphia one of the truest sons Notre Dame has mothered in all her long and glorious history, Mike Powers of the class of '98."

A catcher for the Philadelphia National League club, he practiced medicine with a skill acclaimed by the Philadelphia newspapers quoted by the *Dome*. Because of his moral character he was said to have exercised "almost parental influence" over his big-league mates. They played better when he was in the game, a Philadelphia writer testified, and "they grew in conscientiousness as they associated with him." During his battle with death, the people of Philadelphia demanded and obtained bulletins twice a day from the hospital. Ten thousand mourning admirers walked past his coffin. It was a tribute to his character as much as to his diamond prowess. The leading

Philadelphia daily observed that he was "paid such homage as an eminent statesman or clergyman might receive . . . it was convincing proof of the nobility of baseball that it was able to draw to itself and hold for itself such a man as Dr. Powers."

When Knute Rockne became head football coach and athletic director in 1918, as well as track coach, basketball suffered from wartime attrition of personnel, his disinterest and some ineffectual coaching for a number of years. A dismal record moved the players, more realistic than competent, to hail themselves in self-mockery as "Victory Fives." Under George Keogan in the 1920's the game enjoyed a comeback with All-America players in contention for national recognition. The basketball tradition meantime had been saddled with a sad name inconsistent with the record.

At the end of the nineteenth century varsity basketball had panned out briefly and inauspiciously. But it was impressively revived in the season of 1907-1908 with a schedule of 29 games of which the Gold and Blue won 23. Two of these defeats were inflicted by Wabash College (28-18, 32-15) of Crawfordsville, Indiana. The only team able to defeat the great Little Giants of that season had been Crawfordsville's high school five, the sparkplug of which was center Robert E. "Pete" Vaughan, who in the fall of 1908 joined his former Crawfordsville teammate, Justin "Dud" Moloney, at Notre Dame.

I became an instant fan when the Gold and Blue returned to basketball in 1907. The court was laid out transversely on the dirt floor of the Big Gym, wall to wall, giving it outsize length. I still can visualize James (Laz) Fish that first winter dribbling two-handed from one end of the court to the other. (Downtown we played under Y.M.C.A. rules: for continuous dribbling you had to use only one hand and pass off; to dribble and shoot you had to restrict the dribble to one bounce.) By the rules in force at Notre Dame that first season the out-of-bounds ball belonged to the player who recovered, a rough-and-tumble feature outlawed, I think, the following year. The dribble rule was modified, too, into its present pattern, which requires either a pass-off or a shot when the ball is handled with both hands after a dribble.

Slender, little, dark-haired sophomore Dud Moloney and powerful, auburn-topped freshman Pete Vaughan (slightly over six feet, 190 pounds) were the key stars of the 1908-09 season. Dud specialized in a two-handed banked angle shot as he faded away from the basket along the wall. He was a sharpshooter. The 1909 *Dome*'s basketball review called Vaughan "the whirlwind of the aggregation . . . declared by critics to be one of the best centers in the country. Pete knows the game through and through, and has a unique habit of hitting baskets with opponents clinging to him on all sides." Basketball then wasn't the touch-me-not affair it has become. "In the season," the *Dome* continues, "he averaged more than twice as many goals as the centers who opposed him."

I ran across that item only a few years ago. It confirmed the eyewitness impression of Pete Vaughan as a basketeer which I had formed nearly sixty years ago and have vividly retained.

Thanks in good part to Moloney and Vaughan the 1908-09 season was also a winner. Traveling as far south as New Orleans and Mobile and as far east as Ithaca, New York, to meet Cornell, the Gold and Blue lost only five games all season, two of these to the famous professionals, the incomparable Buffalo Germans.

Knute Rockne's autobiography, published in 1931, but incorporating a series of articles that had appeared in *Collier's* weekly, dispenses the notion that he had never heard of Notre

Dame until some friends persuaded him to take the thousand dollars he'd saved as a postal clerk for years to go there in the fall of 1910. I find it more credible that Notre Dame had yet to hear of Rockne.

He was tentatively committed to Illinois, the story goes, when approached by John Devine and John Plant, whom the biography represents as prospective Notre Dame students, and quotes Rock as asking, "Who did they ever beat?" He should have been able to name someone from his own interest and participation in track. For example, he might have been expected to be aware that Notre Dame had topped Chicago University whenever they competed with others in the same meet. The Gold and Blue's 29 points in the Western Conference Meet in Chicago, June 4, 1910, should have registered with special impact. Two of Notre Dame's first-place winners that day were Chicagoans Forrest Fletcher (hurdles) and Jim Wasson (dashes and broad jump). I'll settle for his obliviousness to the previous two seasons during which Notre Dame won all of its dual meets including a 71-28 rout of Ohio State. But I can't write off the meets with such Chicago clubs as the Central Y.M.C.A., the Illinois A.C., and the Chicago A.A., with one or more of which Rock himself had competed.

The most obvious tip-off of a manuscript textually out of Rockne's firm control is the reported exchange with "Divvy" Devine and John Plant. I'm not sure about Plant—1910 might have been his first year at Notre Dame, along with Rock. But Devine at that time was a veteran of Notre Dame track. Before Notre Dame had heard of Rockne I had seen big Divvy run a record-breaking practice half-mile on the 12-lap track in the Big Gym, and before that he had won his first ND monogram, back in 1907-08 even!

So much for the authenticity of a wisecrack which, against

the background of Rockne's general literary snub of Notre Dame's athletic entity prior to his coming, strengthened when it didn't create a widespread impression that the Notre Dame before Rockne was an athletic nonentity. Let me reiterate my firm belief that this was one of an unfortunate number of collaborative and editorial manipulations of the facts of Rockne's Notre Dame football story made out of ignorance, expedience or carelessness. If Rock had lived longer, I just as firmly believe, he would have righted all misapprehensions. For example, if he did make the belittling remark attributed to him, if it wasn't a writer's invention or a violation of context, then we would have learned that he'd been only ribbing Divvy Devine.

Rock might have credited Coach Fielding H. Yost's postmortem depreciation of Notre Dame's titular defeat of Michigan in the fall of 1909 as "a meaningless practice affair." But, for all his intellectual ingenuity and agility, he couldn't have done that without giving the lie to his implied unawareness of Notre Dame football. I can't imagine his not reading the story of the Michigan game in the Chicago *Tribune* by Walter Eckersall, one of Rockne's boyhood heroes when he quarterbacked the Chicago Maroons. Eckie was one of the experts who recognized the victory over Michigan as tantamount to the Western championship.

For dramatic contrast I could wish it possible to believe both Rockne and Notre Dame had never heard of each other until just before they linked destinies, to go with the indisputable fact that since the meeting fifty-eight years ago the mention of one name inevitably summons the other.

10

To get his degree in engineering, to which he had switched from arts and letters his sophomore year, Red Salmon returned to Notre Dame in 1904 and coached the football team. That season the Gold and Blue, absorbing a 58-0 pasting by Wisconsin, Conference powerhouse, and a 36-0 affront by Purdue, receded from the 9-0-1 peak of 1903 to a 5-3 record. Succeeding Salmon was a brilliant back and whilom end who had been Red's teammate for four seasons. Henry J. was better known as "Fuzzy" McGlew. The nickname was inspired jointly by his great head of tightly curled hair and the prominence in the current newspaper headlines of the British war in North Africa with native warriors called the Fuzzy-wuzzies.

Fuzzy McGlew's '05 team held Wisconsin 21-0, lost to Purdue 32-0, and finished with a 5-4 record. Probably his most impressive contribution to Notre Dame coaching was his part in enrolling Harry "Red" Miller. A few years ago Ray, my closest friend among the Millers, told me that Fuzzy had invited Red to Notre Dame on the strength of a recommendation by my uncle. Uncle Angus never mentioned it, but in his effects I've found a note of thanks signed "Harry Miller." When the first Miller from Defiance came to Notre Dame in the fall of 1906, Fuzzy McGlew had been replaced as coach by Tom Barry of Wisconsin.

Barry's records for 1906 and 1907 were 6-1-0, 6-0-1. Wisconsin was not on his schedule. The Barryites shaved the margin of Indiana's 22-5 scoreboard superiority of 1905 to 12-0 in 1906, and defeated Purdue 2-0. They tied Indiana in 1907 and again turned Purdue back, 17-0.

I no longer can tell the players of this period with any self-assurance of whether I remember them from the field or from the athletic picture gallery in the corridor of the Big Gym. Besides Miller, the names that stand out for one reason or another, most pretty sketchy, are Beacom, Draper, McNerney, Silver, Shaughnessy, Waldorf, Callicrate, Bertling.

I had the most personal reason to remember Bob Bracken, as I'll relate in context with an incident that painfully embarrassed me and, I would learn years later, secretly amused him. It didn't seem possible that I had hated him. I think Pat Beacom, captain of the 1905 team, coached our high school the week of the Big Game. Nathan Silver I identify with some quick dashes in the game he played with a South Bend team against the Physicians and Surgeons of Chicago. I remember Bill Draper in both football and track. Lawrence McNerney I would identify more with alumni reunions although contemporaneously conscious of him as both football and baseball man. I recall "Shag" Shaughnessy, captain of the 1904 football team, most vividly at widely separated points in time and place—first, probably in 1905 when he had a tryout in left field with my uncle's Greenstockings at our Springbrook Park; second, in New York, in 1949 after the Notre Dame-North Carolina game, when he was the long-time president of the International (Baseball) League. Rufus Waldorf (football, 1904, '05, '06)—I was aware of Rufe as a husky football and baseball star with a reputation for rugged competition and rough-and-ready humor: I think he coached the high school eleven a few times. If I had heard he was something less than a dedicated student I wouldn't have been surprised. The fact is that he would be graduated in 1909 with degrees in both mechanical and electrical engineering. John Bertling was identified as the son of a South Bend physician and the older brother of a good little football player who would follow my time in high school.

One of the most colorful and best-liked figures of that decade was Dominic Callicrate. I never saw him play that I recall, yet it always seemed that I did. A few years ago he came back from the West Coast for a reunion and his return reminded a high school teammate of mine that Dom Callicrate had attended the same country school at nearby Granger, Indiana. My friend, Charlie Clemens, several classes behind Callicrate, remembered that he turned cartwheels faster than most of the other kids could run. Nobody could touch him in pom-pom-pullaway. This recall tied in with my contemporary impression that Callicrate was a great open-field runner. Shortly after his visit on the campus, a Holy Cross priest of my acquaintance was assigned to a new church at Granger. When I mentioned that Dom Callicrate, who had been a football celebrity during my boyhood in South Bend, had been schooled in that village, the pastor was reminded that he had heard of Callicrate from a fellow student who had entered the priesthood.

Dominic was teaching and coaching in Portland, Oregon, when young Father O'Malley was assigned to the West Coast with the Holy Cross mission band. At his first meeting Dominic Callicrate was sitting in the front row. The young missioner was gratified for both their sakes, but a little surprised when Dom showed up at another meeting. There was a period when he couldn't conduct a mission without his old schoolmate in the front row. Such devotion in time became disturbingly suspect, until Father realized that in his missionary zeal he had forgotten the young Callicrate's sly sense of humor. He was not so faithfully present solely in search of spiritual rewards, but also in a mood of profane curiosity: to see how many times his former classmate would give the same talk.

Dominic Callicrate was back on the campus again the fall of 1965, with another old-timer, Bill Schmitt of the 1909 Western champions, with whom he followed the Fighting Irish throughout the season. I met and talked with him in the Morris Inn on campus. A straight, tall, still handsome man, alert at or near eighty, easily visualized as the great halfback and the gentle prankster, even as the idol of the country school at Granger.

My most clearly defined image of Notre Dame's football personnel of the first seven seasons of the twentieth century stars Bob Bracken, quarterback in 1904, '05, '06, and captain his last year, as the result of a direct tactical and psychological clash at a South Bend High School practice. He was taking a postgraduate course in law when I was a high school junior not yet released from parental prejudice versus my playing football, but occasionally scrimmaging with the squad without parental countenance. To point up this confrontation I should sketch in some autobiographical matter to illustrate the deep sense of self-importance with which I exposed myself to Bob Bracken's apparent contempt.

We had moved from Michigan Avenue in the autumn of 1907, when I was fifteen, to 111 East Navarre Street, named after Pierre Navarre, pioneer trapper and settler in our parts. John Rittinger, teacher of American history, was the manager of the high school baseball team, but as captain in the spring of 1908, in the fall of which Bracken and I would have our brief showdown, I picked the team and coached it. I had just turned sixteen in February, but my avuncular relationship to the second baseman and manager of the local Central League club (he was one of the circuit's most articulate and colorful figures) bolstered my prestige with the players, some two or three years older. We won all our games, one a memorable 14-inning victory over the more mature Academy nine at Winona, Indiana, and laid claim to the championship of Northern Indiana. Undoubtedly one of my weaknesses was self-consciousness, the dread of appearing ridiculous. It was this egocentricity that would set me up for Bracken's resort to the verbal tactic that deflates. My kind often imagines himself the center of either flattering or unflattering attention when nobody may be paying him the compliment of the slightest attention, pro or con. Conforming with the custom of rising in the morning assembly and reporting from the floor the doings of the baseball team was a recurrent ordeal to which I hadn't become comfortably accustomed. On the other hand, on the athletic field, especially as the chosen leader, I was neither self-conscious nor reticent.

After school I had only to run down the alley the distance of a long city block from the house to be on Leeper Field, where the high school football team practiced every weekday afternoon. I rarely if ever missed a workout, watching or horsing around with other spectators. Our horseplay was simple and not too rough. It's a long time since I've seen one boy sneak on his hands and knees behind another who presently will be dumped by a third. I suppose it's too crude a trick for today's kids. No matter how often we did it, it always could be done again, victim and prankster constantly interchangeable. I associate with the fall of 1908 another pastime in kind except that you could bring it off solo; a simple tactic, yet requiring a knack. You grabbed your man by the shoulders from behind with both hands and if you twisted sharply enough he went flying. The secret of its success was the psychological advantage of surprise. Without it the victim might thwart your game with dead weight. The unexpected seemed to induce a shock that reduced both weight and resistance, or even generated some auxiliary momentum in the direction you meant to spin him. My own immunity to this ambush may have signified correctly that in football I would be more of a dodger than a blocker.

Before Bracken was hired to prepare the Tan and Blue for a key game, the coaching had been done by Ote Romine until he'd earned a suit of clothes. Ote had been a four-sport star at South Bend High, a graduating senior when I made the baseball team in 1907. He had nominated me for the captaincy. A good scholar and debater, the president of the Cleosophic Society, one of the two literary groups into which the student body was divided, he had enrolled at little Wabash College downstate, an institution specializing in arts and letters and an Aboriginal Course in Football conducted by Professor Francis X. Cayou, late of the Carlisle Indian Institute and the University of Illinois. Under Chief Cayou, after-dinner speaker as well as coach, the Wabash footballers became known as the Little Giants, the title reflecting their disdain for odds against them. Typical of Cayou's coaching approach was his method for separating the men from the boys out for their first practice at Wabash. Seating the freshman candidates facing in on a fence encircling a running track he instructed them to grasp the top rail behind them with both hands and lean forward as far as they could without losing their grip. He carried a functional stick. When a candidate was on the verge of letting go, the Chief triggered his release with a sharp rap on the kunckles, tumbling him headfirst into a path of cinders. The next day at football practice time the boys were back in library and lab.

Ote Romine, a slim but sinewy quarterback, had had a season with Cayou before he left Wabash. Ote was tough in his own right, but I think something had been added. I recall an incident that exemplifies my impression. The flying tackle (in much better vogue than its vulnerability to a good straight-arm warranted) was still legal and Coach Romine was much annoyed because he couldn't make his tacklers leave their feet. Although in street clothes, he was goaded by their earthbound reticence to demonstrate, removing only his jacket for the purpose. I can still see him flying through the air to bring the demonstration runner down with a thud. I was one of those who spent the next hour retrieving the parts of his watch scattered over the terrain by the impact.

Toward the close of the season, with the annual Thanksgiving game with Goshen looming, Ote was gone and the captain took charge. I don't recall how it happened that one afternoon I would be caparisoned in that old red turtleneck, a ragged pair of canvas football pants, and elk-hide gymnasium shoes, carrying the ball in scrimmage against the first team. Somebody had given it to me. Dean Myers (Maurice's doughty younger cousin) said, "Follow me" and it turned out to be practical advice. Nobody got in the way and we ran the ball into the street bordering the field on the north. This pattern recurred a number of times. The 1908 team's defense was not considered impregnable, but I was smugly pleased as well as thrilled by my individual showing. I was not modestly surprised. After all, I was not a nobody at South Bend High. Oh, that thing that goes before a fall—I was riding it high.

It was about then that Bob Bracken was engaged to gear the squad to the challenge of the traditional rivalry with Goshen.

Bob Bracken was a handsome, well-built young man of about five-nine in height, 160-plus in weight. My ideal "Notre Dame man" in the life. This was my closest-up look at a gridiron hero out of uniform. He had the air and the carriage—this was the real McCoy, dignified by postgraduate status. No halo, but plenty of aura. Nobody talked about tradition then. Bob Bracken for me was the tradition in person. I hoped he knew who I was—and appreciated the fact that I was the baseball captain, nephew of Aggie Grant of the Greenstockings. Obviously, I didn't respect the one-way perspective of hero worship. If only he'd stick me in to run against the firsts—I'd show 'em up again! I hung around a couple of days without taking part in the practice. But one afternoon the squad was so short-handed that he couldn't muster a defensive line—in fact, until his eye lit on a certain baby-faced little scarecrow, he didn't have enough boys in uniform to man one side of the line.

"Get in there at tackle," he ordered me brusquely.

If he'd added, "you there," I think I would have told my Notre Dame man to go to hell. Under the circumstances, I restricted myself to bitter resentment at being mistaken for an ordinary hanger-on. Me, re-elected to the baseball captaincy—obviously Bracken didn't know my relationship with the Greens. If I was going to play football, the backfield would be my *métier*. No—not even a Notre Dame man could do this to me. But suppose he thought I was yellow. My mind smoldered as I lined up on the spot he pointed out.

Coming my way on the first play was the brother of Harley Kirby, who had played with Salmon: Big Mike to distinguish from Old Mike, his deceased father, and Little Mike, a younger brother. Big Mike added up to about 165 pounds of rawboned power and speed, bearing down on 130 pounds of reluctant cannon fodder. Poor competition, but proud!

I knew what a Poe, a Daly, a Shorty Wilson, any of those mighty mites, not to mention Frank Merriwell, would do in a case like this. But there wasn't time for a picture tackle, shoulder planted firmly in the thigh, lift and drive; or head between the legs, a thigh on each shoulder; in either event, setting Mike back in the direction from which he had fared so confidently, perhaps remembering that I had turned him down as a baseball candidate. I just had time to lower my head for him to run into with a thigh as hard as iron. We sprawled together, me at the inglorious bottom. Mike got up—laughing. My head was ringing as never before in a physical collision. But I was more disturbed by the blow to my vanity of vanities. To distract attention from what I overemphasized as my awkwardness, I remained recumbent, stewing with rage against the dictatorial so-and-so responsible for my predicament. It was an odd time for dignity.

Years later, when I was in Dixon, Illinois, to show pictures of the Notre Dame-Ohio State game of 1935, I met the Honorable Bob Bracken, recently elected or appointed a judge. I was surprised when he said he'd been aware of my background. It had had, of course, no relevance to the situation. He hadn't been sure whether or not I was hurt. But he knew how to find out in a hurry when some of the football regulars quickly and solicitously huddled around me; possibly future baseball candidates.

"Let him lie there," Coach Bracken snapped. "He's not hurt." The calculated contempt in his voice stung me to the core of my ego. That he didn't compound the injury to my person and pride by adding the insult of amused laughter wasn't owing to the lack of cause or urge, he remembered in Dixon. Maybe he was too startled by my reaction. "The hell I'm not hurt!" I yelled, and sprang to my feet in a fury to show that I was. It shocked me a little in Dixon to realize that way deep down I'd nursed a grudge against Bob Bracken, a Notre Dame man in the traditional mold if ever there was one, until we met again nearly thirty years afterwards. No wonder that in this far more complex world of today a psychiatrist and his couch have it made.

Beginning with the season of 1908 the Notre Dame football scene began to come into sharper focus. Names became faces under a thick mat of hair or a headgear; torsos, arms and legs became bodies in uniform on the field. Most of the players who were in on the Western championship of 1909 were around in 1908. I can cite only one who was missing: Al Mertes, two-letter guard, second in a class vote for the graduating student who had done the most for Notre Dame, departed in June, 1909, with a B.S.

Still on deck was Ralph Dimmick, mighty chested powerhouse at tackle and tackle-around. He was probably twenty-two years old when he enrolled at Notre Dame in 1908. He had punched cows in Texas, it was said. I'm not sure which came first in his story, the range or the songs he sang about being on it, accompanying himself on a banjo. He was on the *Scholastic* board of editors.

To look at him, Sam Dolan might have been recruited from a section gang: massive physique, rough-hewn features, stern expression, black bushy hair. He had a bit of wildness in his gaze, I thought. I never saw him smile in the life or in a photograph. His football prowess was as formidable as his mien. He played guard or tackle, carried the ball from either position on "around" plays (in high school, for a reason esoteric to me, we designated the guard-around as the Maple Leaf Play). He backed up the line from the center position on defense, alternating with the fullback. My impression was partly confirmed in a four-line stanza of doggerel in the Notre Dame *Dome* for 1908-1909, before the championship season:

> Sam Dolan is a player of great renown,
> Who scares his opponent with his awful frown.

Tribute in the second couplet is paid to the performance of his duty as prefect of the basement dormitory in Sorin or Corby Hall. I'm sure our—er—poet was aware of the phonetic license he abused when he went on to eulogize Rosy's prefecture as follows:

> He is the big chief of the Hall-house flat,
> And he rules in the subway with great eclat.

Pete Vaughan, nineteen-year-old freshman fullback in 1908, told me years later that "Rosy" Dolan never used vulgarity or profanity by habit. For emphasis he didn't need to. In high and righteous dudgeon he was able to lay about him with a polysyllabic sarcasm that withered. He later became a teacher of English at Portland University. Invited to address an annual Notre Dame alumni dinner, he delighted old grads and new with erudite fluency.

Edward J. "Copper" Lynch was a rugged center who would practice law in Toledo. Another attorney-to-be and big-time collegiate football referee was the late Don Hamilton, quarterback. Husky Mike Moriarity, sub-back, vaulter, quarter-miler and hurdler, general chairman of the Junior Prom committee, second tenor of the Glee Club, was a future priest. Gold Coast (Walsh Hall) Billy Ryan, besides being a dandy football carrier in the open field, was a spitball pitcher, first basso with the Glee Club and star of a campus stage production, *The Hamlet of Broadway*. Billy Ryan was one of the most enjoyable old grads that ever made a reunion—the testimonial is unanimous if my vote will do it. Red Miller, long since retired, had a distinguished career as a corporation lawyer. Bill Schmitt, No. 2 fullback and track man, had substance enough to retire a few years ago, and since has had the leisure and inclination to act as president of the National Monogram Club, follow the football team in season, and between seasons see the world.

A football injury cut short handsome Fay Wood's athletic participation. I never met him then or later, but I indirectly was very aware of his presence. His was the record of a man for all seasons at a men's boarding university, including a couple invested in his LL.B. Besides making letters in football, basketball and track, he wound up as assistant manager of athletics while getting his law degree; he was a member of the Senior Ball committee, treasurer of the 1909 law class, member of the Law Debating Society, president of the New York (State) Notre Dame Club, a sartorial sensation and (the *Dome* makes this official) "a lion among the ladies" of neighboring South Bend and Mishawaka.

No eggheads here by any other name probably; how many, if any, Notre Dame had in those days I wouldn't care to guess: or, to put it more concisely, I wouldn't care. If there were grinds and bookworms, I think they were reasonably integrated with the whole academic and athletic community—the reaction of the *Scholastic* to the conquest of Michigan in 1909 is an exhibit for that judgment, to be cited presently with particulars in the form of an interpretation of that critical event rather than a replay-by-play. In my downtowner's concept of the Notre Dame system, athletics, academic activity and discipline (figured by black-robed Father Joe Burke patrolling the town in horse and buggy) were inseparable.

The Notre Dame athlete I knew most about, without knowing much about any beyond their more obvious athletic records, was our most famous redhead after Lou Salmon, Harry Miller: not only great himself, but the brother and father of Notre Dame greats. Red hit hard on offense, he had great legs, but I associate him more vividly with longer runs. He punted. If he passed for Notre Dame, I didn't know it. But, as in the case of Salmon, I find him potentially a triple-threat back. He didn't play varsity baseball, but he had played and his father had been a member of a famous independent baseball team in Defiance, for which my father had pitched in the twilight of its greatness. All the Millers were well coordinated and versatile, with a special affinity for gymnastics, swimming and diving. I saw Red wrestle in Defiance once during vacation. He and a local youth, known as Jap, toured northwest Ohio putting on mat exhibitions. Red was my hero-Miller. Ray (we called him Tedo) was my summertime buddy when I visited my grandparents. Walter and I were teammates at Notre Dame the fall of 1916—he played excellent football for Notre Dame and would have played even better if he had played more; I always thought that with equal opportunity he would have rated with Notre Dame's greatest halfbacks. Jerry, the fourth Miller brother and the smallest, probably would have emerged the niftiest runner of all if a disability hadn't aborted his football career at Notre Dame. Don's ability and fame as one of the Four Horsemen need no introduction or accolade. Rather, let me render tribute by trying to cut in on the glory. I was still on Cartier Field, weaving around, when he and Jerry were freshmen. I think I once taught Don a practical lesson in defensive downfield alertness against a possible cutback. But my bid for a bit spot in the history of the Four Horsemen (besides having freshman Harry Stuhldreher as roommate) was beating even Don's brothers to the first clear-cut prevision of his future stardom.

If there was one quality evenly distributed among the Miller brothers it was something Frank Leahy hadn't caught onto in his first coaching season at Notre Dame (1941), when Tom Miller was a junior back and Creighton Miller a sophomore. Tom had been a sophomore and Creighton a freshman my last year as an assistant coach under Elmer Layden (1940). These sons of Harry "Red" Miller were both great athletes; Creighton probably was the more versatile and relaxed. In my book he was one of those naturals who take the most formidable challenges in stride. Leahy, a self-driver, misconstrued this ease of effort as thoroughly as you could expect of a master of detail. His most serious blunder was to identify it with a powder-puff personality, a misapprehension probably aggravated by the Millers' tendency to worry him because they didn't. I don't say it was news to Frank Leahy when I said if there was anything a Miller possessed more of than anything else, even over and above superb physical talents, it was *fortitudo*: fortitude, guts. I remember what Frank answered, very reflectively: "I'm glad to know that." I don't know whether he was being surprised or being courteous. The sequel may have been coincidence, but the day wasn't far distant when he would be frankly grateful that the greatest of the football Millers came along in his time.

My first game-action memory of Notre Dame football features Pete Vaughan breaking through the line in 1908 when the coach was Victor Place (Dartmouth, '03), as rugged in person and coaching methods as the New England setting of his playing days.

It would be said of Frank Leahy's coaching formula during the triumphant forties and fifties at Notre Dame that a championship game on Saturday was a picnic compared with the weekday preparatory sessions. From a recurrent point of view inside Cartier Field I would agree in some measure. It was not in jest that his right-hand man, Joe McArdle, was known as Captain Bligh, notwithstanding off-field heart of gold. It appears that Vic Place, with a similar addiction to practice pressures and without a staff of assistants, was his own Captain Bligh.

Red Miller was captain in 1908. He recalls that Place had two well-matched teams he goaded into battering each other so fiercely in intrasquad drills that they were not always up to physical par for some games, as on a Saturday with Wabash. Not that Wabash would have been a pushover under conditions most favorable to Notre Dame. The Little Giants earned their name in 1905 when Chief Cayou was coach by holding Chicago to 15-0, Illinois to 6-0 and Northwestern to 6-0, all within a space of eight days. In 1908 the Little Giants were still mighty and not so little. Notre Dame just bruised by, 8-4. Pete Vaughan, being from Crawfordsville, was familiar with Cayou's tough routine for the college team. The Chief also coached the Crawfordsville High Schoolers—mornings at seven in a world Wordsworth never dreamed of. He was less severe with the youngsters physically. But he made powerful psychological medicine when indicated. And always there was the intriguing dread that the Chief might revert to the tomahawk or knife if his tribe let him down. Pete Vaughan could cite a case in point involving him as principal when he was a fourteen-year-old freshman.

Before a certain game Cayou called a powwow in the dressing room. To emphasize the solemnity of the situation he darkened the room by hanging blankets over the windows. He talked about the creatures of forest and jungle, dramatically citing their habits and respective virtues and vices. The hero of this discourse was the fierce tiger; the villain was the slimy snake. At the climax he shouted, "What are YOU? Tiger or snake?" Every boy present thought the Chief was talking to him alone, fearing for his very life if he didn't measure up to the Indian standard of fortitude.

At least one member of the squad was afraid to interpret the implied threat figuratively. Young Pete Vaughan had made a mistake costing Crawfordsville a touchdown or donating the opponent an advantage. The moment the game was over, he climbed the fence and scuttled for home, literally in fear for his scalp.

At Notre Dame freshman aspirant Pete Vaughan quickly learned that a Dartmouth "Indian" could be at least as hard-nosed as Chief Cayou, the real redskin. His favorite ordeal under fire for a new candidate, especially one who, like Pete, came with a big high school rep, was head-on tackling. As I've indicated in connection with basketball, auburn-haired Pete was no pygmy. Standing a shade over six feet, scaling at least 190, he was heralded as an explosive line plunger with a combative disposition to match. To test his staying powers, Place pitted him against sophomore tackle George Philbrook from Oregon, a weight man and high-jumper in track, fast as well as powerful, packing 220 pounds on a six-foot-six frame.

Big Phil was experienced in the still effective tackle-around run. His instruction was to batter the younger, smaller freshman into quitting. Sophomore end Bob Mathews, dark-maned, glowering Irish-Indian from Fairbanks, Alaska, had taken a fancy to Pete. He assured the freshman that Philbrook could be made to quit first. This was Pete's sustaining thought as he stopped the high-stepping giant again and again, long after he was bruised and bushed enough to call it quits himself many times. (The Indian from Carlisle was a milksop compared with the Indian from Dartmouth!). "He'll quit," Chief Mathews kept telling him. But for this litany of hope, Pete recounts, he would have flunked the acid test long before Philbrook took the seniority privilege of quitting first without losing caste.

The 1909 *Dome*, reviewing the 1908 season, summed up Pete Vaughan's football showing as a freshman in these words: "Not since . . . Salmon has Notre Dame had a man for all-around ability who could measure up to Vaughan. His terrific line plunges, remindful of the famed leader of '03, were irresistable [sic], and his skill in handling the forward pass yielded many a long gain for the varsity." These passes, incidentally, were chiefly thrown to Chief Bob Mathews, hiding with Indian stealth and wile along the sideline.

Vaughan as a linebacker undoubtedly contributed to the Notre Dame defense in 1908 that kept the Michigan offense from passing the Notre Dame 30-yard line. The Wolverines won 12-6 by resorting to the air, but not with forward passes; Coach Yost practiced them, but didn't trust them at game time. The great Allerdice accounted for all their points with his toe. Pete Vaughan galloped 50 yards for Notre Dame's touchdown. P. A. McDonald broke loose for another, but was charged with stepping out of bounds. Captain Red Miller had followed McDonald down the sideline, a little behind and a little to the outside. He never withdrew the opinion that the referee had confused his cleat marks on the line with McDonald's.

Even without Red Miller's unimpeachable testimony I, for one of many, interpreted this 12-6 scoreboard as at least a moral tie. The Gold and Blue would do better than that in 1909.

11

The Gold and Blue star was riding at the zenith of the Indiana college athletic firmament of 1908-1909, according to the following rhymed record appearing in the Notre Dame *Dome* of 1909:

> Let the grinds say what they will,
> They admire both pluck and skill,
> Nay, at times they class as rooters sympathetic;
> When the Varsity wins out,
> E'en the bookworm has to shout,
> There's such magic in victory ath-a-letic.
>
> Reading honors are all right,
> Mental bouts may bring delight,
> There's a keen delicious thrill in beating
> Georgetown at debate,
> But the topmost rung of bliss
> For the college man is this:
> That his Varsity has triumphed o'er all rivals
> in the State.
>
> To the fans of nineteen-nine
> Fate has, sure, been most benign,
> Be their choice of ball or base-, or basket-,
> For the records all agree
> That the gems of U. N. D.
> Glow most brilliant in the State's athletic casket.

On the track or on the field
They've got the goods, and do not yield
One iota of their glory any rival team to freshen;
They are lads to dare and do,
So our good old Gold and Blue
Waves all peerless as it heads the Hoosier
Varsities' Procession.

From the beginning the football varsity had consistently demonstrated lopsided superiority over opponents from schools with comparable numerical enrollment. The presence of high school competition in the early schedules should not be sniffed at. This was a common arrangement to which members of the Western Conference subscribed. Uninhibited by age limitations and academic standards, some of the old-time Preps were up to secondary college caliber. Notre Dame, incidentally, anticipated Illinois and Wisconsin in discontinuing the practice. In the meantime, the first generation of Notre Dame's relations with the Conference, which included Indiana and Purdue, resembled in pattern the pioneer struggles of the institution. The more numerous successes were marred by recurrent unrelieved losses to Chicago, Wisconsin and Michigan, out of which the Gold and Blue battlers salvaged mainly the satisfaction of having taken considerable tuck out of their conquerors, even while enduring their own versions of institutional plague and fire in the shocking form of 54-0 and 58-0 routs inflicted respectively and unexpectedly in 1900 and 1904 by Wisconsin.

Championship aspiration, never dying whatever the prospects or odds, began to enjoy tangible if limited realization in 1901 and 1902 as the Gold and Blue defeated Indiana 18-5 and 11-5 while beating and tying Purdue 12-6 and 6-6. In 1903 Red Salmon captained and coached the team for the second straight season and played the last time. Under his leadership the Gold and Blue, as already noted, enlarged the compass of championship pretension by rolling up 292 points to their nine opponents' zero, a record that included a 0-0 tie with their only Conference opponent, the Wildcats of Northwestern, who had tied the Maroons of Chicago and the Badgers of Wisconsin and edged out the Illini, 12-11. As an undergraduate coach in 1904, Salmon was markedly less successful than in his triple role. From the peak of 1903 the record dipped sharply in 1904 and 1905 (Fuzzy McGlew coaching) with respective win-lose standings of 5 and 3 and 5 and 4, inclusive of the 58-0 walloping (1904) by Wisconsin and decisive reverses by state rivals Purdue, 36-0, 32-0, and Indiana (1905), 22-5.

In 1906, coincident with the introduction of the forward pass as the first potent move toward modernizing the game, Notre Dame took off on a course of championship contention that would be interrupted seriously only once (1933: 3-5-1) in the next half century. The first three-year stage of this epic is significant for the staggered curve upward in state competition:

1906–	Notre Dame,	2;	Purdue,	0.
	Notre Dame,	0;	Indiana,	12.
1907–	Notre Dame,	0;	Indiana,	0.
	Notre Dame,	17;	Purdue,	0.
1908–	Notre Dame,	11;	Indiana,	0.

Up to this point, except for Walter Camp's selection of Red Salmon for his third All-America lineup and professional esteem for Salmon's style in eastern Ohio, recognition of Notre Dame football had been confined to the West—a term designating the athletic Midwest at that time. But as early as 1891 a one-man Notre Dame track team had starred in New York City. The lone contender was Harry M. Jewett, a member of Notre Dame's fledgling football teams of 1887 and 1888 and future automotive designer, organizer and executive.

According to the Notre Dame *Scholastic* (Vol. XIII, 1889-90) Jewett had been the leader of a four-man team in a meet with Michigan at Ann Arbor in May, 1890. The Notre Dame athletic record book credits him with scoring Notre Dame's 13 points. The *Scholastic* specifies first place in the hop-step-and-jump, first in the broad jump, and second by a foot in a 100-yard dash which he lost to John H. Owen, world's champion. Whether this race was run in Owen's record time of 9⅘ seconds is not clear. Frank Menke's *Encyclopedia of Sports* lists Maxwell W. Ford as the world's champion hop-step-and-jumper in 1888 with total distance of 44 feet, 1¾ inches. In 1890 James B. Connolly cleared 44 feet, 10¾ inches —for a new world's record. Perhaps in the interim Jewett's mark of 44 feet, 8¾ inches at the Michigan Invitational stood briefly at the top of the list. In any case, the *Scholastic* represents, he shattered the American record of 41 feet 1½ inches. In the return match the next month, competing in a meet for the Western championship sponsored by the Detroit Athletic Club, Jewett's 10⅕ seconds in the 100 was good enough to beat champion Owen.

All this was prelude to a still more prestigious performance in a meet held by the Manhattan Club of New York. In 1891, running against Cary, the sprint champion of the East, Jewett won the 100 in the record time of 9⅘ seconds and the 220 in the record-setting time of $21\frac{3}{5}$ seconds, which was one-fifth second faster than the previous recorded time made by C. G. Wood of England in 1886.

It was more than a decade before Notre Dame again had an entry on an Eastern track. In 1902 Harley Kirby ran in the Pennsylvania Relays. In the spring of 1908 the Notre Dame baseball team made a swing into New England, and in the winter of 1908-09 the basketball team traveled as far east in New York State as Ithaca, to play Cornell University, and Syracuse, to meet the Syracuse Pastime Club. Now it was the footballers' turn to stage what would be labeled as their first "Eastern Invasion."

The 1909 football season opened with routine romps over Olivet and Rose Poly. Michigan State, the third opponent, had a 5-1-1 record in 1908, including a 0-0 tie with Michigan. When the 1909 season was over, the Aggies had scored 284 points against 33, but none against Notre Dame's 17. It was All Aboard then for the Gold and Blue to play the two Big Games of the Year on successive Saturdays: with Pittsburgh and Michigan.

Downtown we felt that Notre Dame simply was coming into its own in football—that is, into overdue acceptance in the East as championship stock. For me personally the big game would be with Wabash after Pitt and Michigan. That was going to be the only game I would see. High school football was absorbing most of my time out of school in two intimate roles: primarily (at last) as a player; also as sports editor of the school paper and sports correspondent for the *Tribune*. At this point I should take time out to retrace the course of my dual involvement in football.

One of the purposes of this book has been an attempt to interpret the game of football in the life of a youthful participant as an affair of the heart. My own experience naturally is the one I am most qualified to project. I can't pinpoint precisely when and how I decided that I would go out for football in 1909—probably quite a while before I knew it because in winter and spring I was caught up athletically in basketball and baseball, even track. Before entering high school I had never touched the kind of ball with which the basket game is played. Failure to break into what we scrubs dubbed the socially selected lineup of the First Five challenged rather than discouraged my participative interest. Early spring baseball practice at the noon hour merged into another engrossing season and the undisputed if disputable Northern Indiana championship. For me the climax of the athletic year occurred the day of the annual Northern Indiana track and field meet at Notre Dame. I played a game of baseball in the morning on Cartier Field and in the afternoon ran the dashes and broad-jumped.

I'd never worn spiked sprint shoes until I took time off earlier that week from baseball to practice starts in a pair borrowed from a friend who could afford to own them. He extended the loan to include the meet. We anticipated in baseball our overwhelming superiority to La Porte High School in football by defeating them 9-0 that morning in a game featured by our unholy and resistless resort to the squeeze play. I ran two heats in the 100 and the 220 that afternoon, taking first in the short one and second place in the long one, also second in the broad jump. The total of 13 points added up to a bronze medal. This, incidentally, would be my last outdoor track competition until the summer of 1916. By then I was enrolled as a sophomore football and basketball prospect at Notre Dame, but still hanging on to my *Tribune* job and finding time to compete in the city track and field championships for Leeper Park, of which the playground director was Notre Dame's head track coach and football assistant, Knute Rockne.

Before school let out in 1909 I'd taken in all the Central League home games played on Sunday and perhaps a Memorial Day double-header. For a while then I didn't miss a weekday game at Springbrook Park, thanks to passes provided by manager Angus Allen Grant, my uncle. That was an idyl presently burst by manager Donald Angus Grant of the New Sheridan Hotel, my father. He had promoted a job for me. Only reluctantly did I let work interfere with either playing or watching baseball, twin passions whose only comparable rival was my fondness for being in or on one of the three rivers at my old home town of Defiance, Ohio. I didn't mind walking both ways to see a game at Springbrook if I couldn't rake up a nickel or two for carfare. Of course, I should have been grateful when my father set it up with a salesman staying at the Sheridan to pass samples of Bon Ami house to house. For this operation I recruited a team from among my baseball mates. Following that imposition my father committed me to a solo mission tacking up Little Dutch Cleanser signs on barns and fences around the town. This subversion of my vacation increased my impatience to take off on the annual visit in Defiance.

When my second tour of toil terminated coincidentally with the Greenstockings' departure on a road trip, I headed for Defiance; whether with my mother and sister, without them or after them, I don't recall. After moving to South Bend in the spring of 1902 we had never spent less than a month visiting my father's folks. If this time I preceded or followed my mother and sister, the tedious journey by myself, requiring half a day, what with one or two railroad changes on the way, was ideal for reflecting upon my football prospects. But if by then there was any uncertainty about my plans, it concerned the technique of breaking the news to my parents that I couldn't allow my last chance to make a football letter pass me up. I seem not to have been at all daunted by the saturated greenness of my experience or by any doubt of my parents' ultimate surrender to a positive posture. My more immediate concern was to avoid exposing my intention in a premature showdown that would provoke gratuitous discussion.

This undeclared decision did not affect my usual vacation routine except in "piecing" habits. My grandfather's acre had a frontage on the avenue of perhaps 180 feet, two-thirds of it given to a deep lawn adorned by two stately hard maples, a spirelike sweet pear, massive catalpa with one mighty horizontally extended arm from which a rope swing was suspended, a clingstone peach and a couple of sour cherries. I mowed the still considerable expanse of turf at irregular intervals. I might split kindling now and then for the wood-burning cookstove, draw a pail of ice-cold water from the windlass well in the summer kitchen, turn my grandfather's grindstone, or provoke him by my inability to pull a crosscut saw straight back and my tendency to push it toward him. Sometimes I reluctantly allocated precious time to fetching the groceries. The house rambled along a slope steep and long enough to provide swift winter sledding into a spacious bottom piece that dropped off ten or twelve feet to the edge of the Maumee River. I don't remember whether the orchard was still standing that summer. If so, there would have been two kinds of early apple, two trees for cider, a bellflower, a russet (rusty coat), a pair of winesaps, one cooking-eating choice, a dying "rambo," and a wonderful northern spy, besides a shellbark hickory; and I would have thrown many more apples into the river than I bit into, never dreaming that such delicious eating would not be my lot again after this old orchard was gone.

The side lot in front, usually sowed in clover, used to be ample enough for a game of *one o' cat* or scrub. That summer, if anybody showed up for baseball at all, it was to play catch; or, if we mustered three or more, to put on a pepper game. Most often I was out in a heavy skiff rented from a neighbor for twenty-five cents a week. A half mile or less above my grandfather's place was the winding, vine-banked Tiffin River (deserving better than its nickname of Bean Creek) which I might follow a mile or so to the Brunersburg bridge. Oftener I continued perhaps two miles to the Maumee's riffles, sometimes with a lunch, cane fishpole and can of worms. Downriver you could row as far in the general direction of Toledo, Ohio, as the five-mile dam, passing en route the mouth of the Auglaize (which flows into the Maumee at the site of the bluff where Mad Anthony Wayne raised a log blockhouse in 1796) and a recreation spot known descriptively as Island Park, where I first saw some Miller brothers compete in swimming races. On occasion I would explore the Auglaize to its riffles.

There was a swimming hole with a rope almost directly across the Maumee from my grandfather's. Ordinarily I wouldn't dive from a point knee-high above the surface of the water. But the technique of diving off a rope intrigued me. You raise your feet above your head and let go, as any river rat would know, at the top of the swing. The cessation of momentum at that point throws you into a header. The kids I'd played and swum with had mostly grown up and away from the old ways, but it was all right; with my heart set on the football season to come, I enjoyed diving and swimming solo. For variation I once swam and pushed my boat a half mile downstream. I also went swimming a few times in the hole on the Auglaize River with Ray, the No. 2 brother of the Miller football family. "Tedo" had a yard job on which I visited him from time to time to share his privilege of playing on his employers' tennis court.

For about a quarter of a mile north of my grandfather's the residential properties, like his, faced on the avenue and ran down to the river. This provided a wonderful stretch for racing my uncle's Bruce, half beagle, half bull, an ideal running mate. Everything I did in July and August that summer was contained within the framework of my resolution to go out for football in September and my corollary confidence that somehow what I planned would come to pass with my parents' consent because it was such a right thing to do. At the same time I didn't rely on the fitness of my commitment wholly.

For example, since my mother represented at least a psychological block to overcome, I invested our whole vacation together to subversion of her will to resist the appeal of my heartfelt desire. The process, simple and insidious, was a program of ostentatious abstention from confections and pastries at home and of innocently invited attention to my renunciation of Roglietti's chocolate sodas and sundaes downtown. My grandmother contributed both trial and witness to this campaign. She didn't think it possible for young persons to stay long in this world without "piecing" between meals. At least twice a day I had to run out on her sales pitches for the cookie jar. My mother never gave a sign that she knew what I was up to, but she knew I knew she knew—mothers can be like that; certainly mine was.

When South Bend High opened football practice in September, 1909, I drew equipment with the understanding that my candidacy was not to be announced as yet. We had to furnish our own shoes. My elk-hide gym shoes, picked up secondhand, wouldn't wear out. I'd used them for basketball, track and running around Defiance all summer. I'd even swum in them once on a hike when I had the choice of detouring to the Brunersburg bridge or swimming the thirty yards across the Tiffin River near its mouth. After I now had them cleated for football, their light weight and medium-high cut anticipated the modern sprint shoe especially favored by backs. I had in mind going out for quarterback because I doubted my capacity for assimilating and translating the signals into action at game tempo. As a signal caller myself, I would surely remember at least my own number and assignment. On the other hand, I would be competing for this position against veteran quarterback Frank Whitaker, future Western Conference star with Indiana. But the issue was joined and resolved in a way that I could not have invented or divined.

At the time of the first scrimmage I still had not cast the die at home. The first play determined my future positional relationship with football. Lined up at halfback I found myself charged with passing to our right end, down and out. I couldn't spot him. All I could see at the moment was an enveloping wall of linemen closing in on me. I had to get rid of the ball—not to avoid being shaken up, but to escape the humiliation of having to eat the pigskin in my debut as a serious candidate. I was still a personage in my estimation—the two-time baseball captain and medal winner in track.

Desperation sharpened my reflexes. As my eye roved quickly downfield, I detected my fullback, as green as I, who probably should have been blocking for me instead of wandering afield, not sure where he was supposed to be and what he was supposed to do if he located himself. Automatically whipping the ball in his direction, I yelled, "Bon!" It was the best throw I ever made in football. Bon turned just in time for the ball to strike him in the chest. Before he could think and give himself butterfingers, his hands and arms pressed the surprise package to his bosom.

I had hoped my folks would resign themselves to my football commitment if I conducted myself impressively before they caught up with my deception. I hadn't allowed myself to hope that the break would come so soon. Big Mike Kirby, our captain, also acted as coach. Our faculty manager was an ex-Franklin College player, Donald (Biddy) Dushane. Both misinterpreted my instinctive reaction as a split-second intellectual act. When we went to see my father at the hotel after practice it would have been of no avail to endow me with the speed of a deer, the agility of a hare and the ferocity of a tiger. But when they assured him that I possessed the foxiness of a fox, when they said they had to have me for quarterback because of my "headwork," Pop's resistance dissolved into pleased acquiescence. I still can see his gratified grin. Despite his own athletic youth and scrappy nature, my father, like too many parents, never would have given his consent for the simple, basic reason that I wanted to play. In retrospect I think my mother had been reconciled to this development for some time. The incidence of fatal injuries in 1909 would double that of the previous season, but not once did either parent disturb me with a hint of alarm or recantation.

La Porte was a pushover in our first game; we were ahead 60-0 when the game was mercifully called, by the visitors' request, with five minutes to go. In this context I can hardly be accused of boasting if I casually quote my rival high school sports correspondent, Big Art MacDonald, in the South Bend

Times: "Kirby, Boswell and Grant accumulated most of the points, Grant having five touchdowns to his credit through much long-distance running." In my own report to the *Tribune* I appeared only in the summary, an affectation of modesty at the expense of reportorial responsibility.

While making a clean breast of my complicity in the massacre of poor little La Porte, I can render a small service to the verity of football history by citing an added nail in the old fable that Knute Rockne and Gus Dorais veritably invented the forward pass on the beach at Cedar Point, Ohio, in the summer of 1913. When the *Times* reported that "South Bend . . . worked the forward pass repeatedly with success" in a game at Springbrook Park, Indiana, in the fall of 1909, the year before the famous pair entered Notre Dame, it had reference to my "shoestring" pitches to a swift little end named Smith "Doc" Boswell.

We won our second game in 1909 from Michigan City High School, but my self-expectations, blown sky-high by the contribution of La Porte's weakness that year to my first showing, were deflated almost flat on a muddy field. Our third game took us downstate a ways to Culver Military Academy. My ego was somewhat revived when an onside kick bounced nicely into my hands at the safety spot with a clear track ahead to one of the two or three touchdowns we scored while blanking the Culver second team. Afterwards, victory lost some of its flush as we witnessed what might have happened to us had we been booked against the Culver varsity. Paced by the great Yarnell brothers, the first team of Cadets swamped a college team from Michigan. One of the Yarnells treated us to a special spectacle. I still can see him running downfield with the ball in his hand and using it to deliver a devastating straight-arm.

The October 28th sports page of the South Bend *Tribune*

reported preparations for our game that week end at Hammond, Indiana, under this heading:

SQUAD SHOWS PEPPER

Chief of Police McWeeney Puts Snap
into Play of Team

This was the Jim McWeeney who had coached at Notre Dame at the turn of the century. I'd written the story of this workout. But I hadn't included an account of how the Chief's presence had geared a lightweight quarterback into showing off at the expense of genial "Chesty" Littleton. A husky tackle who had exhausted his eligibility, he offered to run from fullback for the scrubs in scrimmage. Chesty stood about six feet, weighed about 180 pounds. I scaled at five feet, seven inches, 133 pounds. But with the Chief looking on, I felt like a little giant. As Chesty hit the tackle hole I met him with my shoulder and rode him back with a crotch hold. He was no Mike Kirby. He ran straight up; you only had to tip him a little and he was going your way. Still, the presence of a personage had stimulated me to show off with more than average zest and authority or I might have been less effective. At any rate, I caught Chief McWeeney's delighted grin with a covert side glance.

The *Tribune*'s lead article that day, of course, was devoted to Notre Dame and Pitt, with a top-deck heading that connoted the eminence of their meeting:

WALTER CAMP AT
PITTSBURG GAME

Greatest Football Critics
Look over Notre Dame

The next two decks of the head and the lead of the story pertained to the previous day's workout at Notre Dame. And then:

> James Deery left today for Pittsburg [sic] to make all arrangements for a special wire from Forbes Field to Notre Dame. On account of classes the students will not be allowed to accompany the team to Pittsburg, but they will be able to get each play over the wire. For the last two years Mr. Deery has been selected to do this thing for the school and always has shown himself to be the best man for the position. The students will collect on Cartier Field and the telegrams will be read to them as they come over the wire....
>
> Walter Camp Will See Game
>
> One notable fact concerning the game Saturday will be the presence of Walter Camp. On account of the showing that Pittsburg has made in the east and Notre Dame has made in the west, he expects to find at least two men for this year's All-American team. Walter Eckersall will also be a spectator at the contest as he is going to pick an All-Western team this year and expects to pick two of the Gold and Blue players.
>
> The team leaves here this evening at 7:45 and will arrive at the Smoky City Friday, at 7 o'clock. The Pittsburg alumni will escort them to the Hotel Schenley in autos. Friday afternoon they will have a short workout on Forbes Field, where the game is to be played. Following the game Saturday, the members of the team will be given a banquet at the Hotel Schenley. After the banquet they will be taken in private cars to the Alvin theater, where both teams will occupy boxes. The theater has been decorated in the colors

of both teams and the management has given over the whole theater to the supporters of the teams.

Sell Seats In Notre Dame Section

Over 5,000 tickets have been sold in the Notre Dame section, of these the Knights of Columbus have taken a block of 2,700. All of the Notre Dame alumni that are anywhere near will be at this game, which will be the first time that the people, of Pittsburg, will be able to see the western style of football.

In those days campus correspondents generally covered Notre Dame practices and home games for the *Tribune*, which published only on weekdays. When the team played abroad, it was up to the sports editor to put together for Monday's paper a report based on clippings and hearsay. A Notre Dame student probably produced the objective piece from which the foregoing extract is reprinted, but I detect the hand of the sports editor in subsequent stories treating the Pittsburgh and Michigan games, before and after the event. He alternately reveals himself as a relative newcomer to the community by his pregame skepticism of Notre Dame's competitive class and his postgame surprise at demonstrations of superiority.

I remember X as a slim little fellow in his early twenties to whom I submitted my high school sports correspondence. His uncritical acceptance of the stuff I turned in, so susceptible to editing of both content and form, reflected in part a personal indifference to local sports, except Central League baseball in and out of season. But it also was the effect of the *Tribune*'s allocation of space to sports news as a debatably expedient concession to the devil. X wrote in anonymity—without the challenge even of an occasional by-line. Moreover, he had a general beat to cover as well as get out a sports section. Perhaps that is at least part of the reason why he passed up play-by-play Western Union returns on Cartier Field. It may also partly account for his negligible knowledge of football's strategy, tactics, techniques and formations. But he was more to be commiserated with than censured. You can believe that. Whatever his faults, including prose that was more distinguished for arid clichés than substance and soared from dull to prim, he did provide a journal of two Notre Dame football firsts: invasion of the East and domination of the West.

I've tried to establish my approach to the history of Notre Dame football as a personal experience in order to preclude any expectation of an objectively documented study in depth, and to that extent absolve myself in advance from competition with professional historian and research specialist.

My conflicting participation in high school football during the historic season of 1909, just before Knute Rockne at Notre Dame, made me largely dependent on the *Tribune*'s coverage of Notre Dame's widely acclaimed emergence as a collegiate gridiron power belatedly recognized. The *Tribune*'s treatment of this phenomenon, although limited in *savoir-faire* and data, contributes a contemporary note to this phase of my personal relationship with place, persons and events. That's a reason for continuing to quote verbatim from the *Tribune*'s sports section in the immediately following pages. There is also the hope that the chronological record of contemporary journalism will help to bring back into focus a traditional image wherever it may have been obscured.

12

The immediate impact of the *Tribune*'s reserved attitude toward the stature of Notre Dame football as it affected me, a high school footballer wrapped up in his own commitment, I don't recall. But in retrospective examination of X's writings on the subject I take instant issue with his reaction to a statement made by Howard Edwards, captain of the team, a local product residing on campus. When Cap Edwards, notable for strength, sagacity and forthrightness, said the Notre Dame team was confident of beating Pittsburgh, he represented the views of players, student body as a whole, and qualified observers. But the text of a midweek *Tribune* article posed that Notre Dame was going "out of its class" in playing Pitt, and heralded this shocking view with a headline that said Captain Edwards was "STRANGELY CONFIDENT." Strangely? That qualification disclosed the sports editor. No campus correspondent would raise such a preposterous doubt. Another tip-off was the inverted lower-case designation of Notre Dame by its colors. Only an outsider would have identified the Gold and Blue as the "blue and gold," a self-betrayal by X of either authorship or editorship.

On Saturday, the day of the game, in an article linking the prospects of Notre Dame vs. Pittsburgh and Michigan vs. Syracuse, X remained skeptical of Notre Dame's chances, but seemed to hedge a little in both heading and text:

GAME DETERMINES MICHIGAN STRENGTH

Yost's Team Meets Strong Syracuse Eleven

ODDS AGAINST NOTRE DAME

Pittsburg's Showing against Indians and Bucknell Makes Smoketown Gridiron Warriors Favorites—Interhall Play

Conjectures on the outcome of the Notre Dame-Pittsburg game were vague and unsettled today. Betting odds showed Pittsburg the favorite. That team's showing against the Carlisle Indians was taken into consideration. Notre Dame's record for this year received attention, but was not considered as brilliant as that of Pittsburg.

If the victory is Notre Dame's there will be every reason for proclaiming Longman's machine one of the greatest in the country. A clear comparison of the strength of Michigan and Notre Dame may be obtained from the results of the "eastern invasion." Michigan plays Syracuse and Pittsburg defeated the Indians. If Syracuse wins from Yost's team and Captain Edwards' men nose out Pittsburg, Notre Dame will rank degrees higher than Michigan.

The "strange confidence" with which X sped Notre Dame to Pittsburgh (changed at game time to an X brand of "stage fright") was quickly converted into a winning touchdown which the *Tribune* reluctantly conceded to Notre Dame under a column-one, four-deck head in the Monday evening paper:

TAKES HIGH RANK FOR SEASON RECORD

Notre Dame Out Plays Pittsburg, Winning 6-0

MICHIGAN COMES BACK

Yost's Team Crushes Syracuse 43-0
Rivals for Saturday's Game Evenly Matched—
Michigan Next

Notre Dame takes rank alongside of Princeton, Dartmouth, Chicago, and Minnesota in the record of 1909 football. Victory Saturday over the Pittsburg team forces praise from critics and plaudits from admirers. The game tried out the staying qualities of the men, the scant margin of one touchdown, made early in the game giving Notre Dame the victory, 6 to 0.

Mathews made the only touchdown of the game. It came early and gave Notre Dame the necessary confidence to over-balance temporary stage fright. Pittsburg was taken aback by the sudden, powerful, and thoroughly modern attack of the western team. Coach Longman's men started with a rush and it was not until late in the first half that Pittsburg rallied. Notre Dame's superiority was proven in the second half when every one of the eleven men came back strong and carried the play into Pittsburg territory to stay.

Coach Longman said before the game that he didn't care whether his team played Yale, Harvard or Pittsburg. "My men are in good condition," he said, "and we are able to present our best front. Pittsburg has one of the best aggregations in the east, but I have no fears for my men."

Coach Longman was one in a hundred, who was willing to predict success. Odds favored the Pittsburg team, two to one, and every angle pointed to a good score in favor of the Smoketown team. The game itself was a revelation to the 7,000 Pittsburg fans, who were surprised to find the westerners adept at the modern game.

Syracuse Swamped by Michigan

Michigan swamped Syracuse under a total score of 43 to 0. The showing made by Yost's men makes it clear that they come back stronger than ever and Michigan is so confident of victory over Notre Dame Saturday they have issued a statement that they expect to win easily. Carlisle Indians defeated Syracuse and Pittsburg won from the Indians.

Interest throughout the west will be more general in the Michigan-Notre Dame game than in the big conference game between Minnesota and Wisconsin. Minnesota is practically certain to win over the Badgers. Michigan and Notre Dame have last year's Allerdice victory* to thrash out and the two teams are well matched. The game will be played in Ann Arbor.

The *Tribune*'s report and remarks are clearly devoid of partisan prejudice. On the contrary, any sentiments that appear to originate downtown, rather than on campus, yield only grudging recognition of the valid championship caliber of the Gold and Blue. Ironically, a dispatch from Pittsburgh conveys a less inhibited impression of the performance against Pitt:

PITTSBURG, Pa., Nov. 3.—Notre Dame's great football machine is still the talk of the fans. Although Pitt's defeat

*Allerdice's three field goals vs. Pete Vaughan's touchdown.

> was a big surprise to its supporters, yet praise goes to the visitors for their great exhibition of the game. In fact, Pittsburg is to be congratulated on the fact that the score was as low as six to nothing. Never since the days of the great D. C. & A. C. and Homestead elevens, with such stars as Fultz, Jackson and Gammens, has a team presented such a bewildering mass of plays as Notre Dame did in this game.
>
> For line-smashing, Vaughn [sic] and Dimmick are voted wonders by the local linesmen. The terrific onslaughts of the visitors' great backfield were just a little too much for the inexperienced Pitt line to withstand the second half, although the locals deserve lots of credit for the way they held when the ball was rushed down to the very shadow of the goal-posts. Left tackle Van Doren and Quarterback Budd are on the hospital list and it is doubtful if they will be able to get in the West Virginia game.
>
> Coach Thompson believes that Notre Dame showed his proteges a lot of things, which will work to their advantage in W. & J. and State game and as these struggles are really what everyone is working for, the Pitt players are by no means discouraged.

In a memoir of the Pitt game, Red Miller notes that Notre Dame's offense was crippled by repeated penalties. One was the charge that the backfield was starting ahead of the snap-back. This could have been a by-product of the "bewildering mass" of plays cited by the Pittsburgh writer, evolving I thought from a tight T type of formation into plunges, fake plunges and runs, spiced with passes, in which fullback Pete Vaughan and tackle Ralph Dimmick were pre-eminent.

Also according to Red Miller, the same official called all the infractions on Notre Dame, more than had been called in all previous games. Quarterback Pete Dwyer was ordered out of the game. He might have been the principal of a story so pat it sounds apocryphal. He was said to have given the offending arbiter a punch to remember him by. His mates with characteristic alertness to the finer points of the game contended that no penalty had been incurred since the blow was delivered by an ineligible player. Not surprisingly, the argument that started on Pitt's 5- or 10-yard line ended on Notre Dame's 45. Whether this was a goal-line stand for which the Pittsburgh dispatch to the South Bend *Tribune* commended the Pitt linemen is not clear.

Single-column halftones of Notre Dame's ground-gaining stars were published in the midweek *Tribune*, apparently provided by a press association with appropriate headings and cutlines as follows:

TORE UP PITTSBURG'S LINE WITH PLUNGES

Vaughn of Notre Dame

Vaughn, Notre Dame fullback, was a big factor in gaining ground in the game with Pitt. His line plunges were irresistible and he was largely instrumental in overpowering Warren, the giant Pitt tackle. Vaughn was pronounced by Walter Eckersall as the greatest fullback in the West and made a great impression on Pittsburg critics. Vaughn is a Crawfordsville, Ind., boy and his friends in that city are watching his great work.

ANOTHER PLUNGER OF NOTRE DAME TEAM

Dimmick of Notre Dame

Notre Dame was continually threatening to score in the game with Pitt and this was due largely to the work of

> Dimmick who gained ground every time he was sent through the line. Dimmick charges like a demon and on a line plunge frequently plows through for five yards and falls by his own impetus. He is 22 years old, weighs 179 [sic] pounds, and is playing his second year on the team.

Notre Dame lost Pete Vaughan by transfer in 1910 to Princeton. From 1912 to 1916 he was assistant football coach and head basketball coach at Purdue. Called into active service on the Mexican border in 1916 with Company C, 152nd Infantry, Indiana National Guard, he coached the Camp Shelby (Mississippi) football team the fall of 1917. Shortly before the Armistice in 1918 he went overseas as commanding officer of Company C, and remained in France long enough to coach a divisional team in the A.E.F. spring football championships. Beginning with the fall of 1919, he coached football and basketball and intermittently headed the department of athletics at Wabash College for nearly thirty years. His lively interest in the academic activities of his athletes was recognized when Wabash awarded him an honorary M.A. In 1966 Wabash established the annual *Pete Vaughan Award* to the school's outstanding athlete of the year. At the same time, as an honorary alumnus, he received the *Award of Merit* made annually by Wabash alumni for distinguished "attainments in professional, educational, political, military or other fields, in keeping with the high purposes of Wabash College."

An inveterate student of football, Pete experimented with a variety of offensive and defensive formations, tactical combinations and sequences. He has followed the game closely in retirement. Obviously there have been things on his mind since 1909 besides the Pitt game. I was prepared to be advised that he couldn't disentangle the details of that occasion from the mesh of conflicting memories of gridiron action in which he had participated directly or indirectly for so long. But after I had finished the first draft of this book I appealed to Pete (July 5, 1967) as follows:

"For my little book about Notre Dame before Rockne, I wrote mostly out of memory, but had occasion to dig back into the South Bend newspaper files with special reference to the 1909 season. Sports in general didn't get the detailed play they are accorded today, of course, but I bumped into some interesting material which I had forgotten, recalled faintly or hadn't been aware of.

"You may be able to clarify one point for me out of your memory. After the Pitt game of 1909 the Pittsburgh papers raved about Notre Dame's deception. I guessed that you must have used some T formation stuff along with punt formation in order to account for the befuddlement of the Pitt reporters. Can you reconcile their reaction with reasons why?

"For a long time I've had the impression that Ralph Dimmick was older than the average of the squad and that he used to sing cowboy songs and accompany himself. Correct?

"If you could enlighten me in these areas, at your earliest convenience, it would be helpful."

Seventy-seven-year-old Pete Vaughan doesn't write with the ease of old. It was a tribute to our camaraderie of fifty years that on July 10 I received two laconic communications of data in the same envelope that bring into sharp focus the discrepancy between the close score and Notre Dame's domination of the Pitt game. Here they are, verbatim:

July 6

Dear Chet:

Ralph Dimmick came from a famous family in Washington or Oregon, some state in the Northwest. The family were big ranchers. When Dim was a teen-ager some of the cowboys went to the Argentine and Dim went with them. When some of them went to Australia Dim came back home. He got a job on the railroad and worked up to conductor. Then his folks talked him into going to school. So Dim entered Parsons Academy of Whitman College. The academy men were allowed to play on the college team. Later Dim, Mathews, Philbrook and Martin (track man) entered N.D. Dim worked hard at his law classes. On the trips he carried two suitcases—one for his personal equipment and the other filled with books.

He was quite a character, Chet. He learned Spanish when in the Argentine, played the mandolin (I think) and sang thru his nose the cowboy songs (many in Spanish).

Every once in a while he would go to the N.D. farm. Ride a horse, shoot his gun (he was a good shot), and lasso some of the cows. Also he would use the flying balls—sling them around his head—let them go and catch the cows by the legs.

(Come to think about it I never saw him at the farm. But I heard all about it, so that sometimes I think I saw him perform. But I'm sure I did not.)

Dim's brother became governor of Washington (it was Washington or Oregon) and when Dim died his brother wrote me. I was at Princeton at the time.

I was a frosh at N.D. Just out of High School and had never been away from home—and then I met Dim. I was under his feet all the time, always wanting to hear his stories and his songs. He was a great guy. We corresponded until he died. He dictated a letter to his nurse, which came after he died. If I start writing about Dimmick I'll never get on with this letter.

It is midnight. So I'll quit and finish this tomorrow.

Pete.

July 7.

Dear Chet:

I got started on Dimmick. He was a great guy, Chet, and I missed him when I went to Princeton.

As for the Pitt-N.D. game . . . As I remember it we received the K.O., ran it back to about the 30-yard line. Went into a spread punt formation. I was the punter. Faked a punt, ran the end for 1st down. Then same thing to the left. Another 1st down. Then faked the punt, faked the run and threw to Mathews, who was in the clear and scored. This was the first minute or so.

We used close formation, Right & Left, Q.B. under center. We ran their ends, hit off the tackles, used reverses and tackle-around plays. Dim could carry that ball. But we could not score again.

Once I went off tackle, cut in and only the quarterback was in my way. I straight-armed him and went all the way. But the officials said I hit him with a closed hand and penalized us for unnecessary roughness—15 yards from the spot. We spread our ends and just before the ball was snapped they would come in and line up regular. We had the ball on the 5-yard line. I faked in, jumped and passed to Mathews, who stayed out that time. He caught the ball and *stepped* over the goal-line. But the official ruled he *caught* the ball over the goal-line, so it was a touchback. [There was no end zone in 1909.] Pete Dwyer was our Q. B. at that time and he protested so vehemently the official put him out of the game. And so the game went on.

Dim got the squad together and said we can't score but we can work on a couple of Pitt's men that have taken advantage of the officiating. One big tackle–named Van Horn*–made it rough on the N.D. end and tackle. So Dim said, "Run the tackle-smash at him." So we did and in a few minutes Van Horn* was carried off. Dim turned and said, "Pete, you shouldn't have hit him that hard." And from then on every Pitt sub came in shaking his fist at me. And Dim would just laugh.

We used the quarter under center. Don Hamilton made numerous quick passes to the ends who cut out or in as planned. And we quick-kicked from regular formation.

One time I was with Don Hamilton in Columbus, Ohio. I had gotten the N.D. formation mixed up with others. So Don straightened me out in lots of details.

My memory plays me tricks. I never talked over the '08 and '09 seasons with a teammate except that time in Columbus. And after Don told me his memory of things, lots of it came back to me. But it has been such a long time that I could have it all wrong. I hope not.

Pete

In the winter of 1916–17 Notre Dame was playing Depauw in basketball. Company C had been demobilized. Pete Vaughan came over to Greencastle from Crawfordsville to

*Van Doren

see the game. I met him for the first time. I think he recalled my name in connection with South Bend High School athletic competition. At that time he must have noticed that while Notre Dame was having its difficulties with the officials at Pittsburgh, our high school had had a postgame skirmish with some hoodlums at Hammond, Indiana. It's unlikely that he knew that the story of the game and its unscheduled sequel in the *Tribune* was mine. Nor would he or anybody else who read my write-up have guessed that I started this riot in a teapot. Adjoining the Notre Dame-Pitt four-deck lead story in the *Tribune* of November 1 was the following three-decker:

ANOTHER STEP IN MARCH TO TITLE

South Bend High Defeats Hammond Handily

Drunken Hoodlums Try To Rough It with Members of Team—Football Warriors Hold Their Own

South Bend High took one more step toward the Northern Indiana championship Saturday by defeating Hammond High at Hammond, 11 to 0. On the whole the work of the representatives of the "tan and blue" was good, although at critical times there were some bad fumbles which cost South Bend several chances to score. Loose defensive work was also noticeable in the second half. Buechner and Richter, South Bend's two tackles, played their best game of the season, the former being the first man down on every punt, while Richter broke through time and time again and downed his man for a loss. Nicar and Clemens played good defensive games, while Kirby and Whitaker "skinned" tackle for long gains again and again. Boswell, Wolf and Berkey at ends usually broke up the plays around their ends, and received their forward passes well. For Hammond, Captain Kennedy put up the best defensive game, while Ayres, quarterback, got his forward passes off accurately and sent off some long punts.

On the way to the street car depot after the game, the South Bend boys had a set-to with some half-drunk hoodlums, who claimed to have lost some money on the game. . . .

I've quoted the *Tribune*'s report of the game in full partly to make restitution, nearly sixty years overdue, for the omission from the text of any reference to our two valiant guards, Marcel Walsh and Ed "Cupid" Gross. Chiefly I would again explain why the name of quarterback Grant appeared only in lineup and summary although another sweetly bouncing onside kick by the opponent had been convertible without obstruction into a long touchdown run. I had two reasons for excluding its mention from the lead, neither identifiable with modesty, true or false. First, in my eyes it represented at best only a partial redemption of an otherwise unsatisfactory personal showing. Second, I made a point all season of ducking around any printed self-recognition that conceivably would expose me to charge or suspicion of impairing *esprit de corps*.

I had another kind of reason for not disclosing the identity of the "football warrior" who struck the blow that started the concert after the main show. My account in general purposely veiled and garbled the details in order to avoid even the implication that some of our sturdier warriors had exhibited touching but censurable faith in my ability to get myself out of a ticklish situation I'd got myself into. Some of the funny things that happened on the way to the depot couldn't be encompassed in a typical stick or two of *Tribune* type. This was too good a story not to be told until now—and I suffered privately from self-inflicted reticence.

I don't think our harassers were drunk. They may have lost a buck on the game. But chiefly, I believe, our straggling column of out-of-town athletes offered too tempting game for these lovers of tough sport to pass up. Four or five of us were cut off from the main body by a passing freight. Ken Berkey and I brought up the rear. The fun began when a little ruffian—probably in his mid-twenties; he looked old to me—grabbed Berkey by the shoulder. Our great end, not fearfully but wisely, shrugged the fellow off and went on. The hood then laid an arresting hand on me. I've read recently in Dwight D. Eisenhower's memoirs that as a boy he liked to fight. That suggests one of several reasons why, although born in Ohio, I didn't grow up to be President. It was only when I was deeply affronted, by unfriendly contact or a nasty name, that I struck out. In this instance I was irked into shooting a straight left to the nose of the offender. When he tried to close in on me, I apparently dropped my suitcase. The next thing I knew I was standing with feet widespread, more like a wrestler than a boxer, with both hands clenched, facing a solid semicircle of what appeared to be amused noncombatants. The whereabouts of my erstwhile adversary remains an unsolved mystery.

The rage—or alarm—that caused my blackout had subsided. My honor had been satisfied. All I wanted now was to retrieve what I perceived to be a missing suitcase and march on. I didn't have to look for it. It came hurtling to the edge of the crowd. Its specific target was another unresolved question. One Don Kale, South Bend football follower, had picked it up and let fly for good luck or bad. (Over my shoulder I saw that two or three of our big boys were huddled against the crossing gate.) For all I ever would know, it was Berkey who routed my man. The first punch was all I could consciously claim.

At the moment I was more concerned about forestalling the necessity of throwing another. As I penetrated the crowd a step or two for my case, I indicted its hurler distinctly and placatingly: "That was a hell of a thing to do!" I wanted all to know whose side I was on right then. Another appropriate tactic for the moment was to keep my head and eyes lowered in order to insure no exchange of direct glances that might be interpreted as a challenge.

By that time the gates were rising. Presently I caught Louie Wolf, still wearing knickers, and Big Mike Kirby. A wee person in a black derby hat accosted Big Mike. A fighting fool on a football field, Big Mike was all good nature off. As he turned with a big friendly grin, the accoster smacked him alongside the head, with two remarkable results. Big Mike sailed sideways the full width of a fifteen-foot sidewalk. He was physically all right, but his feelings were hurt. Turning on his assailant, he demanded in loud, aggrieved tones, "Now what did you want to go and do that for?" If I'd been tempted to throw my suitcase myself this time, Mike's rhetorical reprisal invalidated that gesture. But Little Louie, whose hulking shoulders belied his youth, charged the derby hat and he faded into our mobile gallery—chuckling, I'm sure.

Pretty soon Louie and I found ourselves in the company of Clarence "Mul" Williams of South Bend, former high school football star who had refereed our game. I don't know how we got clear of the crowd and commotion. With a gesture that boded ill for the next molester, Mul showed us the section of a car spring he had picked up. Just then we heard a shout from the rear, "Get the guy with the car spring." If our pursuers found the spring, there was no guy with it. Mul hadn't waited for a second notice to prompt him to throw it up the nearest alley.

Soon another little hood having fun overtook us. Irritated perhaps because he detected no provocative weapon in our possession, he ran at Louie, took a poke at him, and withdrew hurriedly as Lou came back at him with his case, then dropped it in order to free both fists. I had to high-tackle and wrestle our pugnacious freshman end out of the notion of pursuit. Meantime, Mul had kept going. But he must have met the enemy after all before attaining the sanctuary of the station. When we arrived, our entire South Bend group was assembled, safe, sound and unmarked (even Big Mike) except Mul Williams, who was sporting a black eye he hadn't had when last we'd seen him.

Despite my strong personal engagement in the football action of 1909, I followed Notre Dame's fortunes with unabated concern and confidence. I imagine that I was more disappointed by the close Pitt score than elated by a victory I never doubted would be Notre Dame's. If I gave any thought to X's blue notes in the *Tribune*, it had to be derogative of his capacity to judge.

That was a weekend during which anybody's triumph was darkened by the shadow of tragedy. Three deaths on the gridiron, raising the season's total to eleven, were reported. The hue and cry against college football, largely muted when mass formations were banned and the forward pass legalized, was heard again. Leaders of higher education, however, reacted generally in defense of the game. When the commandant of the United States Military Academy suspended the schedule at West Point for the season, the action was construed as a "tribute of respect for the memory" of one of the day's victims, Cadet Eugene A. Byrne. Among those national figures who declined to be stampeded into condemning the game out of hand were the head of the United States Naval Academy at Annapolis, the Army Chief of Staff, and the presidents of Minnesota, Northwestern and Notre Dame.

I still recall the day in high school assembly when the Rev. John W. Cavanaugh, C.S.C. bound a typically restive crowd of students in the spell of his eloquence. Since football had become a varsity sport at Notre Dame, he was the third successive nonathletic president who recognized the rough game as a traditionally integrated phase of life at this school for boys and men. He made a statement published in the *Tribune*. Evidently commenting on blue-nosed hysteria, he is quoted as having said, with calm understanding and foresight:

> "Spasms of virtue do not help. Football to-day is a less violent form of amusement than it ever has been before. The unfortunate accidents to these young men will not occasion any important change in the manner of playing the game. Boys have found a way of perishing even when football has not been played.
>
> "I venture to say that more people have died of pneumonia, contracted while viewing a game, than have lost their lives on the field playing it. I believe, too, that there are many times more deaths from automobile accidents than there are from football.
>
> "Nothing particular will happen as the result of these unfortunate casualties."

This candid evaluation of the situation might hit some readers as a callous dismissal of the tragic incidence of football. Not at all. It was simply a realistic confrontation of a hard truth. Rough males will play rough games with or without official countenance; the institution renders a practical and moral service by providing instruction and supervision. Everybody was for making the game as safe as possible.

My recollection is that at least the University of Notre Dame and South Bend High School played out the season without losing a single man to parent or reformer.

13

While we South Bend High Schoolers were getting ready to host a "highly heralded" team from Huntington, Indiana, at Springbrook Park, we followed Notre Dame's preparation for Michigan in the papers. I'll try to resist the temptation to interpret some of the advance reports in the perspective of history, and by this self-imposed discipline preserve more of the contemporaneous mood, which is the reason for quoting headline and text literally, beginning with the *Tribune* of November 3, 1909:

SCRUB WITH WINGS TRIED OUT AT HALF

Moriarity, Speed Merchant, May Oppose Michigan

ENDS PRACTICE BLOCKING

Allerdice's Punts Will Cause Trouble Unless Collins and Mathews Hold Well—Examinations Bother Longman

Moriarity, a scrub with winged feet, was tried out at halfback on the Notre Dame varsity yesterday afternoon, following up a plan by Coach Longman, which he expects to use against Michigan. Moriarity (varsity hurdler and quarter-miler) is the fastest man on the scrubs and can pass any of the varsity. His forte is on end runs. He can circle the ends so fast that he gains at least five or ten yards before a defensive end or quarter can run out to intercept him. Longman is of the opinion that he will be a good man to put in the game in the second half after the opponents have been tired out.

McDonald was used for this style of work last year and always made good. It was his end runs that won the game with Marquette last year. The scheme is one that is not successively [sic] combatted and Moriarity will be given a chance to show his speed in the game with Michigan. Several new plays were tried yesterday afternoon and were run off quite smoothly. The plays are much different than any of those that Notre Dame has used this year. Coach Longman has seen Michigan play twice this year and has a fair idea of their plays while the coaches from Ann Arbor have not been able to get a line on the Notre Dame plays.

Fear Allerdice Punts

Allerdice, the Indianapolis boy, captain and halfback, of the Michigan team, is the peer of any punter in the west and if Collins and Mathews cannot block Yost's speedy ends Michigan will continually gain ground on exchanging punts. Longman gave his ends a long drill at blocking and impressed on them the importance of stopping the opposing ends. This discrepancy is the only fault in the work of Collins and Mathews.

Examinations Cause Trouble

Examinations are giving Coach Longman much trouble coming as they do just before the most important game of the year. Not all the men were able to be out and practice was largely devoted to signals. The men are in fair shape with the exception of Miller and Dwyer. Dwyer is suffering from his injured knee and may not be able to get in the game against Michigan.

The campus correspondent would have written the foregoing piece on Tuesday. It appeared in Wednesday's paper. On the same page the following Ann Arbor dispatch contradicted his assumption that Michigan had not scouted Notre Dame:

COACH WATCHED GAME

Michigan Man Says Yost's Men Will Have to Play Hard

ANN ARBOR, Mich., Nov. 3.—Notre Dame, coached by Frank Longman, star fullback during the seasons of '04 and '05, will be the next adversary of the men of Yost. They will begin the game, as other teams have begun games against the yellow [maize?] and blue already this year, with the expectation of "doing" Michigan.

Saturday Notre Dame kept their season's slate clean by finishing ahead of Pittsburg in a 6 to 0 battle, and the western teams came through the fracas in the best of shape. Coach Prentiss Douglas of Michigan's freshman team, visited the Smoky City to get a line on "Shorty's" squad, and returns to Ann Arbor with the conviction, win or lose, the Wolverines will know they have been through a football game by Saturday evening.

"The Hoosiers play football all the time," said Douglas, concerning the Notre Dame eleven, "and they go as far as any team can go without calling forth penalties for roughing from the officials. As last year they have a star backfield, heavy, fast and game, and their offense is better than anything we've yet run into."

Another Ann Arbor dispatch appearing in the South Bend *Tribune* the day of the game indicated that Michigan's supporters hadn't read or didn't believe Coach Douglas' warning and had discounted the pattern of Michigan's 12-6 victory in 1908.

WOLVERINES CONFIDENT

Defeat of Syracuse Makes Rooters Look for Big Score

ANN ARBOR, Mich., Nov. 6.–Memories of the decisive defeat of Syracuse University last Saturday by Michigan eleven led their supporters to expect a large score against Notre Dame on Ferry Field today. Injuries from which several of the Indiana players are suffering were expected to weaken the visiting eleven.

Coach Yost, however, strongly cautioned his men against an overdose of confidence and hinted at an unexpected strength in the Notre Dame team.

Notre Dame supporters expected the punting ability of Fullback Vaughan to play a large part in the showing they hoped for from their eleven. Capt. Edwards, of the Indiana team, is suffering from a carbuncle on his knee and it is considered doubtful whether he would be able to play more than a part of the game. Following is the probable lineup:

Notre Dame		Michigan
	Left End	
Mathews		Borleske
	Left Tackle	
Edwards (Capt.)		Casey
	Left Guard	
Philbrook		Benbrook
	Center	
Lynch		Watkins
	Right Guard	

Dolan .... Smith

Right Tackle

Dimmick .... Wells

Right End

Collins .... Miller

Quarterback

Hamilton .... Wasmund

Left Halfback

Miller .... Magidsohn

Right Halfback

Ryan .... (Capt.) Allerdice

Fullback

Vaughn .... Clark

If Coach Yost regarded the Notre Dame threat as worthy of no more than a hint, it appears that he disregarded both the futility of his 1908 ground attack against Notre Dame and the warning in his 1909 Notre Dame-Pitt scouting report. The South Bend *Tribune* on the same day ventured no forecast. But the head and text of Sports Editor X's article, without prophesying, registers the expectation that Michigan will win:

INDIANA WATCHES GAME AT MICHIGAN

Notre Dame-Wolverine Contest Attracts Attention

YOST'S ELEVEN FAVORITES

Defeat of Syracuse by Big Score Gives Ann Arbor Team Odds–Fullback Vaughn Carries Hoosier Hopes

All Indiana is watching the Notre Dame-Michigan game at Ann Arbor, Mich., this afternoon. Most of Indiana is rooting for Notre Dame. A few Michigan alumni are pulling for the Wolverines. There is no doubt but that the game is the most important contest in the west. The Chicago-Northwestern game had been cast into the shadow by the interest in the struggle between teams coached by "Hurry-up" Yost and "Shorty" Longman.

Michigan is the favorite for the victory. Yost's powerful eleven ran up an unexpected score on Syracuse last Saturday, showing that his men are capable of coping with the best in the east or west. Allerdice is a tower of strength for the Ann Arbor team. His kicking ability alone makes a point in favor of Michigan that is not offset by the playing of any Notre Dame player.

In the line Michigan is sure to break up a great deal of Notre Dame's successful line plunging. Casey and Benbrook cannot be handled with any degree of certainty. Borleske and Miller are wonderful ends. In the backfield every man is a star in his position with the exception of Wasmund. The little quarterback lacks several necessary qualities of the field general.

Vaughn Holds Notre Dame Hopes

For Notre Dame Vaughn will be depended on to do the best work. He is an important cog in the forward pass system and starts many of the trick plays. He is also likely to do the punting. Dimmick, Hamilton, Miller, and Mathews, are the other mainstays of the scoring machine. Capt. Edwards is not likely to get into the game on account of his bad leg.

The result of the game will have an important bearing on the western championship. Michigan later plays Minnesota

> and Minnesota is conceded the conference title. Should Notre Dame win it will be entitled to consideration at the end of the season as a claimant of the championship. Michigan also plays Pennsylvania and a clean slate before that game will make the Wolverines confident of victory over the Red and Blue.

I don't remember precisely when our high school football team received the flash of Notre Dame's win over Michigan. I know that the news lightened the gloomy wake of a game of our own that we didn't win. Between the distractions of my disappointment by a sorry stalemate with Huntington (Indiana) High School and my elation over Notre Dame's decisive victory, I put off writing the story of our game for the *Tribune* until Monday morning. Not until then did I realize that I didn't know the name of the big back who had scored both Huntington touchdowns—on long runs during which I, as our safety man, had had the regrettable distinction of missing the last tackle. It had been a highly heralded game, spectacularly played. But I just had time before school to dash off and deliver a flimsy report that didn't deserve this paltry pica headline:

SOUTH BEND AND HUNTINGTON TIE, 12-12

Demon of Visiting High School Eleven Is Star of Game

"Demon" was the truly descriptive alias by which I identified Mickey Erhardt, future all-conference football star at Indiana. Monday evening, still brooding over my defensive contributions to Huntington's two scores, flinching at the thought of my reportorial fake, I still could enjoy the *Tribune*'s appreciation of the Notre Dame-Michigan affair. The coverage, however, was typically inadequate, as the verbatim textual record illustrates under this heading:

NOTRE DAME TAKES HIGH RANK IN WEST

Defeats Michigan 11 to 3 by Brilliant Work

IS POWERFUL MACHINE

Coach "Shorty" Longman's Squad on Par with Minnesota and Wisconsin, Leaders in Conference
—Corby vs. St. Joseph

Football experts throughout the west are singing the praises of "Shorty" Longman's band of Notre Dame moleskin warriors, who by defeating the Michigan team 11 to 3 Saturday, put in a strong bid for the western football title. Those who saw the game declared that Yost's team displayed a reversal of form over the brilliant showing of the preceding Saturday. A writer in the Chicago *Record-Herald* says that Notre Dame "literally mopped up the field with the maize and blue." Walter Eckersall, of the Chicago *Tribune*, declares that Notre Dame has earned the right to be classed with Minnesota and Wisconsin, leaders in the conference.

Rooters returning from Ferry Field are united in their criticism of Quarterback Wasmund's generalship against Notre Dame. On many occasions it is said that the Michigan field master employed tactics tending to aid the visitors. The Wolverines apparently displayed a woeful lack of "pepper."

Notre Dame maintained a brilliant irresistible chain of banging, rushing drives against the Michigan forwards, resorting to the forward pass in pinches and always getting away for long gains through the medium. With the defeat went Michigan's chance for copping the western championship, for Notre Dame now is rated one of the most powerful machines in the western country.

Students Celebrate Victory

The entire student body celebrated the victory of the Notre Dame football team over the Michigan squad with a huge bon-fire on the Brownson campus Saturday evening. Speeches eulogizing the members of the Notre Dame team were made by members of the faculty and representatives of the student body. Among those who made speeches were Rev. Timothy Murphy, prefect of discipline; Father Carroll for the *Scholastic*; Father Irwin for Corby; Father Burke for Sorin; Brother Hugh for Brownson; A. J. Cooke and J. B. Murphy for Old College; James Deavitt, athletic manager for Brownson Hall. The entire demonstration was under the superintendence of James E. Deary.

While the returns were being read to the students on Cartier Field Saturday, Corby and St. Joseph halls played the fourth game of the interhall series. The game was the most spectacular of any of the present series. . . . Both teams used the new style of football quite frequently and brought forth much applause. . . .

Details trickled to us through various media. Everybody knew Red Miller's running had been sensational. The concentration of pregame attention on Pete Vaughan had set up the scene for Longman's new plays featuring Miller. I've read in a book that Red carried the ball ten straight times to Michigan's two-yard line. This I don't understand. Such a drive against Michigan by a Notre Dame redhead was bound to have been compared with another great march by that earlier redhead, Lou Salmon, and I don't think I'd have forgotten if it had been. According to the *Tribune*, Pete Vaughan took the ball over from the eight-yard line. I'll settle for around the three- or four-yard line because the going was so tough that quarterback Don Hamilton resorted to high-pressure psychology that might have backfired if Pete Vaughan had been less dedicated to his role in the game.

Pete told me the story many years later when I was doing a magazine story about him as a veteran coach at Wabash College. At the time he was reported as having exploded through the line with such force that he broke the goal post with his head. That's the way Father Matthew Walsh always told it when he was vice-president of Notre Dame. Pete rejected the implication of hard-headedness. He was sure that he hit the post with his shoulder for the reason that he didn't feel the impact. By some quirk of his nervous system he was almost immune to pain in the area of his shoulder. "If I'd struck home with my head," he said, "I'd have known it. It had to be my shoulder." But that was incident to what happened between him and Hamilton. Just after calling the last plunge, the quarterback turned and snarled, "Come on, you yellow-backed so-and-so!" Pete's next thought after scoring was to annihilate the libeler. He had chased the laughing quarterback half way upfield before he realized that Hamilton had capitalized on his hair-trigger temper.

The score was 5-0 when Michigan recovered its onside kick deep in Notre Dame's territory. Unable, as throughout the 1908 game, to break through the Notre Dame defense, Allerdice place-kicked for three points. Score, 5-3.

Only once more was the Notre Dame goal menaced. The Wolverines recovered a fumble on the Notre Dame two-yard line. Unable to crack Notre Dame's goal-line stand on the first two downs, the Wolverines lined up for a field-goal attempt. There had been a discussion. Quarterback Wasmund, it was learned later, wanted to go for it. Captain Allerdice overruled him. The students in the stands called for the toe that had been good for all Michigan's scoring on Notre Dame in 1908: four kicks, 12 points. Three points here would put the Wolverines out in front 6-5. It looked like a sure thing, and most likely was just that except for a factor over which the kicker had no control: the potential capacity of the opposition to block even a perfectly timed kick.

Red Miller draws the picture. The whole line ready to rush: Mathews, Edwards, Philbrook, Lynch, Dolan, Dimmick, Collins. "Each man was set, like a tiger about to spring, his body taut, his face grim, his lips drawn back, his teeth flashing: a picture of power and determination." Then, the snapback of the ball; the entire Notre Dame line charging. Boom. Boom. Kick and block. The ball bounds back 35 yards. Sam Dolan falls on it. It's almost anticlimactic when, soon after, Billy Ryan runs 30 yards through a broken field for the second touchdown. Notre Dame, 11; Michigan, 3.

That's the way it stood at the end of the game, but it was Notre Dame all the way home. Red Miller almost broke loose for another score. Quarterback Wasmund, playing safety, nailed the Notre Dame flyer by the ankle. Later Miller had a clear field ahead when he lost Pete Vaughan's 40-yard pass in the sun. Chief Mathews, running with Miller, got his hands on the ball and carried it across the goal, but the throw was ruled incomplete.

Newspaper writers as far east as Boston in various forms corroborated the judgment of a Cleveland expert who classed the 1909 Notre Dame team as "probably the cream of the country."

In the cold light of the Monday after, when he realized that

Notre Dame had been both expertly and popularly awarded the distinction he coveted for Michigan, "Hurry-up" Yost said, according to the Chicago *Record-Herald*, "You must recognize that we went into the game caring little whether we won or lost."

But when his more honest emotions prevailed and spontaneous judgment dictated an expression of opinion, he testified as Notre Dame's most qualified if reluctant booster. In this mood he made the following remarkable, perhaps hysterical admission:

"What makes me so doggone mad is that we might have won. These are the worst kind of games to lose. They leave a worm in the heart to gnaw and gnaw. O, I don't know. I'm sick and tired of the whole business. It certainly is discouraging. I take my hat off to the Irishmen. They are regular Indians. I was afraid of them because they have all the qualities of great players." The implication of this last remark might be that he had underestimated his former pupil's ability to take advantage of exceptional playing talent.

I hope he also said, as elsewhere quoted, "It was certainly a treat and took away some of the sting of defeat to watch that redheaded Irishman shake 'em off," having reference to an Irish-German named Miller. Such praise would have been warranted, but might be apocryphal. Red himself testifies that Yost charged him with signaling for fair catches in an unsportsmanlike manner when his men were not alert enough to avert the contacts for which they were penalized.

By and large, the great Michigan coach, forever renowned for his point-a-minute teams, was mainly concerned with minimizing the significance of his Wolverines' clear-cut defeat. The famous Chicago *Tribune* columnist HEK, neatly wrapped up Yost's obsessive depreciation of the game when he wrote, "Nothing, it seems, remains to make the disparagement of Notre Dame's victory over Michigan convincing but the declaration (by Yost) that Michigan never did play Notre Dame."

By the time the *Scholastic* went to press, Michigan had defeated Minnesota, Conference leader, leaving Notre Dame the indisputable champion of the West. An upset tie in the final game with Marquette dimmed the prestige of the title perhaps, but doesn't nullify an exercise in comparative scores. This is a popular resort for those whose side profits by the comparison. Without advocating as a finalizing authority this method of rating football teams with championship contenders they haven't contended with, I found it interesting to note that the statistics in this case were one-sided in Notre Dame's favor.

Syracuse provides the common denominator of a contest of statistical comparison with Yale, the Eastern champion. Yale beat Syracuse by 15-0. Michigan beat Syracuse by 43-0. Even the old-fashioned mathematical process of subtraction is competent to show Michigan comparatively superior to Yale by 28 points. Throw these into the hopper with Notre Dame's eight-point margin over Michigan, and by this or any other method of computation the reading is: Yale, 0; Notre Dame, 36. Fair enough!

Today the *Scholastic* issues preseason and postseason special editions on varsity football—in bad years as well as good, let's note. In 1909 virtually an entire regular issue was devoted to hailing the Western champions. Less than a page was allotted other matter in order to exemplify and dramatize "the totality of enthusiasm" with which Notre Dame traditionally identified with any and all of its representative projects.

Of the fourteen undergraduate members of the *Scholastic*

board of editors, I can identify the first eight listed. All but one were future priests and distinguished educators. The exception was a newspaper man, Dennis A. Morrison. I knew Denny Morrison as a South Bend *Times* reporter when we both were very young. The others were Peter A. Hebert, Michael A. Mathis, Thomas A. Lahey, Francis Wenninger, Charles Miltner, John F. O'Hara and George Finnigan. From this group would emerge, besides excellent teachers, a missionary, two college deans, a bishop and a prince of the Church.

The front cover of the football issue celebrated in the inevitable verse the acquisition of the championship of the West and the determination to perpetuate its possession, as these typical stanzas indicate:

'Twas an all-star bunch of players,
They were hustlers, also stayers,—
Played the game from start to finish with enthusiastic zest;
They could be, at need, good losers,
But the good old Gold and Blue, sirs,
Was not losing, not exactly; we were
Champions of the West.

Did our rooter-clans foregather?
Did they whoop it up? Well, rather.
Why, the welkin needed mending at the close of every test;
And—a fact of common knowledge—
Football simply owned the college
When the varsity got home at last, the
Champions of the West.

Take it from me straight, nay, rigid,
That the day will be some frigid
When our foes dislodge the title we are hugging to our breast;
As we have it, so we'll hold it

On our banner we have scrolled it,
And the Gold and Blue henceforward spells the
Champions of the West.

The first two inside pages, plus a half-column runover, are assigned to a review of all "big games" on the Notre Dame record since 1887. Next are three pertinent pieces of additional verse. Two are satires: 1) "Yost's Practice Game," a lampoon on "Hurry-up Fielding, the hard-nosed loser"; 2) "The Parable of Drawing the Line," recording the Michigan Goliath's plaint that his contest with Notre Dame's David was all in fun. According to the vanquished giant, the little stone-slinger hadn't played fair. I've mislaid the serious set of rhymes, along with some notes pertaining to a two-page section of individual tributes to the members of the squad and the coaching staff, illustrated by a full-length shot of Captain Edwards, a group picture of the sixteen-man squad, head-and-shoulders photo of "manager and assistant coach" Curtis, and a one-column overall view of head coach "Shorty" Longman in uniform and three-striped Michigan sweater identifying him as a player with three of Michigan's greatest football teams. I remember mainly about the text that it was signed "—J. F. O'H.," the initials of the late John Cardinal O'Hara.

A lead editorial, "Hail and Farewell," is addressed to members of the graduating group of veterans and recognizes their submission to institutional authority without submersion of individuality in an appropriate if somewhat stilted appreciation: "In the intoxication of its great victories and in the excitement of congratulations, there is one point which is apt to be overlooked, but which appeals to the student of men as uppermost; this year's team is an aggregation of individuals, and if it worked well as a machine—and few machines harmonize more perfectly—it was because each man put the best of his individuality into his work, and considered his team-mates as well as himself."

Cap Edwards, "when asked what he had to say regarding the Michigan game," expressed the *Scholastic*'s thought less rhetorically. "It was great," he said. "Every one of the men fought and fought like demons all through the game. Everybody starred and they should receive the same praise."

The theme of a second *Scholastic* editorial carried the satirical heading: "Mr. Yost Didn't Care." This was a variation in prose of the versified version of the contradiction between Mr. Yost's obvious respect for Notre Dame's football prowess on one side of his mouth and on the other his attempt to depreciate the titular significance of Notre Dame's triumph over his Michigan.

On the page facing the editorials we find "the concept of the celebrated cartoonist Packard" of Notre Dame's championship, sentimentally interpreted as a gift by the team to the school and symbolized by the figure of a football player on his knees handing up the world, in the form of a globe-map, to a charming young woman bearing an ND pennant.

"Championship Gossip" heads a little over two pages of six-point type required to accommodate quotations from the press hailing Notre Dame's irrevocable title to the Western championship and favoring a claim, by comparison of scores, to the national leadership. Quoted are the South Bend *News* (where, O where, was Sports Editor X of the South Bend *Tribune* when the smoke cleared?), the Indianapolis *News*, the Indianapolis *Star*, the *Inter-Ocean* and the *Tribune* (Chicago), the *Post* and *Times-Star* (Cincinnati), and the Boston *American*. The *Scholastic* editors demonstrated, however, that they hadn't lost their total perspective, even for a glorious edition, by interpolating in a column of campus notes this injunction, apparently written in advance of the Marquette game: "In the flush of victory and the overindulgence in championships, let it not be forgotten that Corby also won."

There is also the promise that the next issue will include, besides an account of the "0-0 dogfight" with Marquette, "a report of the Corby-Brownson game, in which the former won the interhall championship; the selection of an All-Interhall Team; and an account of the (student) reception given the Western Champions on their return from Milwaukee."

Nonathletic items in the football issue included favorable mention of a concert in Washington Hall by the Gembel Concert Company; notice that a steam-pump company in Holyoke, Mass., "wants to hear from a graduate of the mechanical engineering course at Notre Dame"; an editorial from the *Catholic Transcript* of Hartford, Conn., commending Notre Dame "for having taken the lead among Catholic schools of learning in providing a course in aviation."

The athletic-academic relationship was further indicated by the announcement that a committee of class presidents will sponsor "a worthy tribute to the team that won the Western Championship," in the form of "a banquet to be given to the victors by the entire body of collegiate students."

This was the climate of the Notre Dame that Knute Rockne found, not founded, in 1910: an environment uniquely favorable to the development of high-class athletic groups, complementing and integrating with the general educative process.

14

I gavc notice at the outset of this memoir of Notre Dame football that I would try to conjure up the pioneer era before Rockne as an experience in which I participated as a figure involved with the game in spirit and act and with the institution in appreciation. My research has been limited. Red Millei and Bill Schmitt of the 1909 champions are frequent campus visitors within short walking distance of my residence. Pete Vaughan's letters about Ralph Dimmick and the Pitt game sample the possibilities if I should undertake at some future date a more objective study of these old times while these three articulate old-timers are still accessible. But my approach to the matter at hand will continue to be subjective.

In 1909 my perspective on the contemporary scene was that of a senior high school student and football player. My reactions to direct and indirect exposure to the Notre Dame football action naturally were conditioned by my own involvement in athletics at a lower level of age and performance. For example, I can't recall visual evidence of a shoestring forward pass thrown by Pete Vaughan to Chief Mathews. But I could and can visualize pattern and technique of their execution of this maneuver from parallel personal experience. On the day that Notre Dame was beating Michigan, partly through forward passes or the threat thereof, I repeatedly called the shoestring against Huntington, with uncommon effect thanks to our bowlegged little right end, Smith "Doc" Boswell. Hiding out along the sideline as the teams lined up for scrimmage, he would sprint straight downfield at the snap-back of the ball. I was not an accurate passer like Pete Vaughan. I made no effort even to sight my man. I simply threw as far and high as I could, down and out. The rest was up to Doc, running with controlled speed in order to adapt himself to the height and range of the arc.

In the Notre Dame-Wabash game I saw the Notre Dame quarterback, Don Hamilton, make a legal forward pass after crossing the line of scrimmage, yet I doubt that I'd trust my own memory of this phenomenon peculiar to this one season had not a bizarre personal experience in kind led to one of our two touchdowns against the same Huntington. I had signaled for a shoestring pass but for some reason elected to run. I was perhaps 25 yards downfield when one of the demon Erhardt brothers bore down from a bad angle for me. To elude him I needed an assist from a straight-arm; otherwise, he was big and fierce enough to break me in two, I thought. But in the attempt to fend him off I was in peril of fumbling away a good gain. In other words, I wanted no part of the Erhardt family. In fear for both self and charge, and with faith in my unseen Boswell on the right flank (his respect for star billing was not the least of his competitive assets), I broke my stride just enough to get rid of my hazardous burden high and far, dead ahead. If it was humanly possible, even if it wasn't, I knew that this miniscule prefigure of Superman would never let the ball drop. Sure enough, here he came, bolting to my rescue; his short shanks blurred by the speed with which he pumped them, he made the catch on Huntington's 30-yard line and raced to a TD: a ground, air and ground maneuver covering about 85 yards.

I'm sure that in the fall of 1909 the state of Wisconsin domiciled a future Notre Dame quarterback already capable of exploiting the forward pass with far more skill and warranted success than mine. His name was Charles Dorais. At the same time there was a mail dispatcher in Chicago who hadn't played any football to mention since quitting high school about the year that the forward pass was legalized. His name was Knute Rockne. Entering Notre Dame in 1910, "Gus" Dorais quickly registered as a naturally great passer, runner and kicker. It was not until 1913 that his teammate, Knute Rockne, of the same class, was identified notably with the passing game. Because of a dramatic and novel display of aerial strategy and tactics against Army that year by the Dorais-to-Rockne combination, these two became popularly but erroneously acclaimed as forward passing pioneers.

While the 1909 Notre Dame team was winning a scrimmage with Miami (Ohio) University 46 to 0 (November 13), South Bend High was losing a controversial game at Warsaw by forfeiture when Capt. Kirby withdrew us from the field in protest against a homegrown referee's interpretation of two legitimate touchdown dives as illegal hurdles, with Warsaw leading by 12 to 11. Except for an errant forward pass that probably would have won the game for us despite what we branded as partisan officiating, my personal showing was the most enjoyable since my pyrotechnical debut against hapless La Porte. Warsaw made a familiar miscue against us, a faulty onside kick, low and to one side. As before, I had only to field it on the first bounce in order to transport it into a touchdown without human impediment. More satisfying were some zigzag runs from scrimmage, effective enough to make the crowd yell, "Get that quarterback!" The sequence I recall most definitively elicited a vocal demonstration remindful of how thin the veneer of civilization separating the group hysteria of the modern sports buff from the thumbs-up-thumbs-down mob mood of the Roman rooter at the outmoded gladiatorial spectacle.

I started left and cut right. The Warsaw right tackle, I assume, was blocked in. The right end was a stocky, tow-headed kid wearing no helmet. I left him at his post. Angling to my right, I dodged and gained until shut off along the right sideline. There I was forced into an attempted double reverse of the field and might have got clear but for the persistence of that Warsaw right end, whose delight was pursuit—of me in particular. This wasn't the first time he'd missed the initial tackle on one side of the field and showed up inopportunely on the other. He wore a triumphant little leer the last time he lunged and broke through the open hand I had thrust into his broad face. This time the partisans, crowding the sideline, howled and shrilled, "Kill that quarterback!" This, of course, was inversely complimentary. I got up laughing and so did my nemesis. It was all in the game.

At Monday's practice following the Warsaw incident Farmer Geyer, subguard, accidentally stepped on my right instep. The pain was sharp and sickening. There's a commemorating lump on my metatarsus. For a moment I was in the mood to strike in sympathy with the Big Eight faculty representatives who were planning "to vote dangerous football off the western gridiron." But this I shook off in the heat of working out, only to make the dismaying discovery that I had become allergic to defensive contact. Specifically, I couldn't bring myself to tackle below the waist.

This embarrassing inhibition could have evolved in part from frustration by my demon, Mickey Erhardt. The score was 12 to 0 in our favor in the second half when he took the ball on the kickoff and broke through. I was our last man. He outweighed me by 50 pounds. I should have maneuvered him out of bounds or slowed him down until help came. Instead, I played him dead-on, giving him the last critical move to either side. He stranded me with an immobilizing hip fake combined with a sharp sidestep or cross-over. I barely broke his stride with a desperate arm tackle. When he got loose once again, I repeated my blunder. My chagrin over this double disaster was deep-seated and lingering, possibly inducing loss of confidence in my tackling ability. I hadn't been tested defensively at Warsaw. When my tackle-shyness showed up I didn't know I was also coming down with the grip. So I resorted to a whack at the tackling dummy as a possible cure for tackleitis.

Every Thursday was "Girls' Night" at practice, which was highlighted by a drill in tackling the dummy on the fly. Our dummy was a sad sack of sawdust set up on end. There was no pit, but it didn't hurt if you made the proper connection; the sack absorbed most of the concussion. Our feminine gallery stimulated us to compete for distance. The target looked mighty small and the gap from the projected takeoff was frightening. It was only the chance to show off that overcame my own moment of dread as I lined up for the run in an attempt to outdo the best previous effort. Now, in a private show I found I still wasn't afraid to leave my feet a reasonable distance at a relatively soft, motionless, sawdust torso. But when I returned to the field I still shied from hurling myself at a live, moving target with arms and legs. We were scheduled to play at Dowagiac, Michigan, on Friday. I don't know which had come first, worry about my funk or my touch of influenza. At any rate, I didn't make the trip. But nothing could keep me from attending the Notre Dame-Wabash game on Saturday.

We expected Notre Dame to win, of course, even with Vaughan, Ryan, Dwyer and Dimmick sidelined. But we all had admired the Little Giants, at least from the time that Chief Cayou had made them the talk of the West. They chronically gave the Gold and Blue a sharp battle no matter what the adverse odds of prediction. We high schoolers had reasons more personal for empathy with the Little Giants. South Bend's only representative on the 1909 eleven was Cap Edwards. South Bend High had been represented at Wabash by Buddy Harris, Bob Rowe and Ote Romine. We had followed with sectional interest the Wabash career of the great Starbuck from Goshen High, our annual Thanksgiving Day rival. Four members of our current squad would play for Wabash within a year or two. Others had their eyes on Purdue, Indiana and assorted colleges of the Midwest. Big Mike Kirby would enter Wabash and transfer successively to Purdue and Princeton, not knowing that Notre Dame had taken him for granted because his brother Harley had been a Gold and Blue track and football star and because he, Mike, had worked out with the varsity track athletes. I entertained no collegiate prospects or intentions, athletic or academic. Of all my 1909 high school teammates only Louie Wolf would enter Notre Dame from high school and he would major in baseball. The common attitude toward Notre Dame's athletic tradition and record was one of respect and admiration. I certify myself as a 100% devotee. But I, too, might have gone to Wabash if I hadn't been away playing bush league baseball when Wabash coach Jesse C. Harper was in South Bend asking about me in the summer of 1912, by suggestion of some of my former high school mates who by then were playing football under Harper. The next year he was at Notre Dame, and two years later he would offer me an athletic ride.

The *Tribune* of November 18, 1909, printed the following dispatch from Crawfordsville:

WABASH READY FOR FRAY

Strongest Team on Field Against Notre Dame

CRAWFORDSVILLE, Ind., Nov. 18.–South Bend football enthusiasts who see Saturday's clash between the Little Giants, of Wabash College, and the mighty Notre Dame University, will witness a battle royal. The Wabash eleven is in fine fettle for the fray.

The freshman members of the eleven have not been in a game since Hanover was defeated 48 to 0 by Wabash Oct. 30. The men eligible under the conference ruling, which Wabash was forced to observe, when she played Purdue University, have had a rest of two weeks. The fact that the Little Giants, minus their freshmen and four-year men, trounced the fast Purdue eleven 18 to 7 [my records give Purdue 17 points] at Lafayette, demonstrates the strength and speed of the Wabash collegians. The team that lines up against Notre Dame Saturday will be stronger than that which defeated the Boilermakers. While Wabash does not expect to win from Notre Dame, her players are determined to make a splendid showing and to hold the Notre Dames to a low score. They realize that it would mean much to Wabash to be able to hold the north state bunch.

Wabash has been coached this year by Jesse C. Harper, the former University of Chicago star. Harper started the season with a squad of about 35 men, all of whom were new and inexperienced. By careful coaching and stupendous work, he has developed an eleven, which, although light in weight, is exceedingly speedy. The team averages only 160

> pounds and has no man weighing more than 180 pounds. Spectators at Saturday's game may look for some spectacular work on their part. This year's eleven is particularly noted for its low, hard, diving tackles that have been characteristic of every team that has represented the Presbyterian college for the past half dozen years. The players follow the ball closely while the ends are whirlwinds in getting down the field on punts. Although light, the line is strong, both offensively and defensively.
>
> The last time Wabash and Notre Dame played football in South Bend, Wabash was victorious by a score of 5 to 0. Last fall Notre Dame came to Crawfordsville and won a close victory 8 to 4 (all points scored on field goals, counting 4 each that year). The game was one of the hardest fought in which Notre Dame took part that fall.

Accepting this estimate of the Little Giants' potential prowess, we expected them to serve as foils challenging enough to make Notre Dame perform impressively and we weren't disappointed. Meeting Captain Mike Kirby downtown, we rode the Hill Street trolley to the southern edge of the Notre Dame property, walked a rutty half-mile to the entrance of the quadrangle, at the other end of which stood the twin-winged golden-domed brick administration 'building dating back to the Great Fire of '79, and then cut across a hall recreation field, past the Big Gym, to Cartier Field with its high board fence. The Notre Dame *Scholastic* records that the weather was a bit chilly and windy for the cross-country team that day. But as I recall the afternoon of November 20, 1909, it was ideal for football. Certainly for us, with the Dome glistening under an Indian summer kind of sky, it was a red-letter day in a gold and blue setting. The South Bend *Tribune* of that date corroborates my impression and the Monday *Tribune* reports that a record-breaking crowd enjoyed both game and weather.

Looking over a picture of this squad recently, the members individually unidentified, I was able to pick out and name every man at a glance save James Maloney, end—from New Upper Falls, Massachusetts, I learned from the Directory of Monogram Winners. I could visualize most of them in action. The predominance of names obviously or possibly Celtic reminded me that Notre Dame teams didn't acquire popular identification as the "Fighting Irish" until the cross section of Irish nomenclature had notably diminished. A rundown of the lettermen of 1909 in this picture and their home towns reaffirms the traditional national scope of Notre Dame's enrollment.

In the line from end to end, we see, besides Jim Maloney, Robert Mathews of Fairbanks, Alaska; Howard Edwards, South Bend, Indiana; George Philbrook, Olympia, Washington; Edwin Lynch, Toledo, Ohio; Samuel Dolan, Albany, Oregon; Ralph Dimmick, Hubbard, Oregon; Luke Kelly and Joseph Collins, Boston, Massachusetts. Behind the line: Donald Hamilton, Columbus, Ohio; Albert Kelly, Morris, Illinois; Billy Ryan, Cleveland, Ohio; Harry Miller, Defiance, Ohio; William Schmitt, St. Paul, Minnesota; Robert Vaughan, Crawfordsville, Indiana; Peter Dwyer, Syracuse, New York; Michael Moriarity, Ashtabula, Ohio, not shown in the picture, would run the Wabash ends for gains of five and ten yards when substituted for Red Miller. Four of those named above would be on the sidelines with injuries: Dimmick, Ryan, Vaughan and Dwyer.

I entered the gate to Cartier Field that day only five-foot seven; I exited with my head scraping the sky. There was new authority the next week when I called signals. I've never forgotten the loud, firm, confidence-breeding tone of jut-jawed Don Hamilton's signal-calling voice. The two-handed basketball kind of forward pass he made downfield while in the grasp of an opponent is my reference point in college football when the 1909 rules are in question. I was disappointed that my No. 1 hero, Pete Vaughan, was benched, but the pounds-lighter Bill Schmitt cracked the Wabash line for exciting gains and the No. 2 subject of my worship, Red Miller, ran inspiringly. Again and again it was only one man who prevented him and Don Hamilton from going the whole distance on breakaway runs. The *Tribune* identified him for me as Hawkins, the Wabash quarterback.

I think it was Red Miller's last run that remains etched most vividly in my memory. I see him taking his stance in long punt formation, prepared to kick or canter. The ball is on or near the Wabash 45-yard line. Red's left foot is forward, his body inclined slightly forward from the waist, hands extended. It's a sweep to his right, toward the sidelines where I stand. His good knee action doesn't impair his speed as he slants his course slightly before changing direction downfield off his right foot. Little Giants are closing in from his left in a sort of staggered column. The first one makes his bid just as Red turns the corner. He doesn't lay a finger on the striding redhead. He goes down as if pole-axed and that virtually is what happens to one would-be tackler after another: letting go at the runner with all the famed Wabash-trained abandon only to be struck down by the heel of Red Miller's fending left hand, quarterback Hawkins among them if he was still in the game. Red Miller's path to this touchdown is strewn with Little Giants.

The *Tribune* made special mention of runs by Captain

Edwards, Albert "Red" Kelly, subbing for Billy Ryan and Pete Dwyer, and Bill Schmitt for Vaughan. Edwards and Philbrook scored a touchdown each, whether out of the line or from fullback, the *Tribune* doesn't say and I don't remember. Besides running cleverly, Hamilton kicked all points after touchdown and placed one for three points from the Wabash 45. Other touchdown scorers were Schmitt, 1; Miller, 2; Red Kelly, 1. Maloney at end is the only defensive standout for Notre Dame the *Tribune* mentions. Obviously, the defense as a whole was adequate in a game won, 38-0.

The sight of Red Miller's explosive straight-arm transported me to heroic heights of planned emulation of offense against Goshen, and at the same time wrought a practical miracle in my defensive reflexes. On the way home from the game, footing it, I had to restrain myself from tackling every telephone pole and hitching post I came to. I could scarcely wait until Monday to try out my transformed tackling complex on human objects.

The *Tribune*'s sports section usually carried a masthead across the top of the page. On Monday, November 22, it was displaced by the following six-column ribbon:

NOTRE DAME PROCLAIMED WESTERN CHAMPION

The story of the Wabash game was made up in the sixth column. The banner story in the first column, headline and text, should be read in context with recollection of sports editor X's "show me" posture before both the Pitt and the Michigan games; also in similarly corrective context with the popular impression that athletic Notre Dame at this time was an intercollegiate unknown:

NOTRE DAME WINS CHAMPIONSHIP

Honors Secure since Michigan Defeats Minnesota

YOST ADVANCES CLAIMS

Says Wolverines Played Hoosiers for Practice, Eckersall writes "Results Count"—Steffen Selects All-Western

Since Michigan's defeat of Minnesota, the Notre Dame football team has a clear title to the western championship honors and only the most biased prejudice can deny Notre Dame the honors. They have gone through the season without defeat, and among their games, they list a victory over the mighty Wolverines. The latter's defeat of the Gophers leaves nothing in the path of Notre Dame's title as champions of the west.

This fact is recognized by Walter H. Eckersall, one of the best informed authorities in the country. Writing in Sunday's Chicago *Tribune* he says: "By winning a decisive victory (over Minnesota, 15-6), Michigan is entitled to be ranked as one of the strongest teams in the west. If it were not for their defeat by Notre Dame, they would be the undisputed champions of the west."

In this morning's *Tribune* Mr. Eckersall states: "In the west Notre Dame must be considered the logical champion because the Hoosiers defeated Michigan earlier in the season and the Wolverines in turn trounced Minnesota, the champions of the western conference."

MICHIGAN CLAIMS TITLE

Fielding H. Yost and the Michigan players to a man are claiming the western title. They do so on the ground that

Notre Dame is not a conference team and does not observe conference rules.

"Of course we are champions," said Yost in an interview in Minneapolis. "What else did we come up here for, but to carry away a title. It is well enough to put Notre Dame in as a claimant, but that doesn't get the Hoosiers anything. They don't approach either of the conference teams in eligibility rules. We took on the Indiana team because we needed work, and we got it, all right. But as for any championship claim at Notre Dame, that doesn't go at all. There are men on the Notre Dame team who have played years beyond the recognized limit in the west, so that bars them. They have a good team down there, but you must recognize the fact that we went into the game caring little whether we won or lost. Practice was what we wanted."

The Wolverines and their great coach seem to have forgotten that it has been several years since they have been within the fold of the western conference. Minnesota is the champion of that association because it holds a clear record of victories in its games with other members. By defeating the Gophers, Michigan has taken away from them the credit of being western champions and in turn the Wolverines have lost that honor to Notre Dame; as Eckersall states in his article of this morning, "results count and Notre Dame should be given full credit for its achievement."

"Sour Grapes"—Perhaps

The statement that Michigan went into the game simply for practice makes no difference in the final result. That the coach of an amateur team, playing for the sport there is in the game and for the honor of the college it represents, can claim that team cared not whether it won or lost a game, seems incredible. It is far from sportsmanlike to say the least and looks on the surface like a case of "sour grapes!"

That Notre Dame is the western champion there can be no gainsaying. Figures cannot be juggled to make a defeat appear a victory and when all is said and done the score of the Michigan-Notre Dame game stands as indisputable proof of the claim of the Hoosiers.

Two Notre Dame men are given places on the mythical All-Western eleven selected by Wallie Steffen, the All-American quarter who starred last year for Chicago and who is now writing for the Chicago *Examiner*. The favored Hoosiers are Dimmick at left tackle and Vaughan at fullback. Speaking of Dimmick, the writer says: "He has earned a place on the team by his splendid, consistent work. No end has been able to box him and no consistent gains have been made over him. He is clever in advancing the ball; once underway he is difficult to stop." Regarding Vaughan, Steffen writes, "He is the strongest back of the season. Without the assistance of halfbacks he has been able to tear large holes in the opposing lines. As an interferer he has no superior in the west."

Other members of Steffens' star cast are: Page, Chicago, right end; Walker, Minnesota, right tackle; Butzer, Illinois, right guard; Badenoch, Chicago, center; Dean, Wisconsin, left end; McGovern, Minnesota, quarterback; Allerdice, Michigan, right halfback; Rosenwald, Michigan, left halfback.

Not everybody from Michigan took the Notre Dame game as lightly as the coach did after losing it. For example, if they had viewed it as a practice game, South Bend's Michigan rooters conceivably would not have returned from Ann Arbor berating the Wolverines' field generalship cantankerously and categorically, as reported in the *Tribune*. It seems incongruous that a mere workout would have exposed the Michigan field general to censure by Michigan fans in Ann Arbor so rabid and unfair that the sympathy of his opponents was enlisted. ". . . the only thing the players feel bad about," the *Tribune* campus correspondent reported upon their return to school, "was the way that Wasmund, the Michigan quarterback, is being spoken of." The *Tribune* printed a special dispatch pointing up and dramatizing the extremity of the bitterness aroused by the "practice" defeat for which Wasmund was being excoriated:

EXONERATES WASMUND

Capt. Allerdice, of Michigan, Issues Signed Statement

ANN ARBOR, Mich., Nov. 9—Capt. Allerdice issued a statement last night exonerating Wasmund from all blame in connection with the play that is supposed to have caused Michigan's defeat on Saturday at the hands of Notre Dame.

"Whatever error of judgment was committed," said the leader of the Wolverines, "was my error and not Wasmund's. The defeat hurt, of course, and I probably feel more badly about it than anyone else. I thought the place kick was the proper play and tried it. It failed and we lost. Wasmund was in no way to blame."

I'm sure I can reconstruct some of the reactions outside of Michigan to Yost's outburst after the Minnesota game. In the role of the coach who didn't care, Yost's performance was acclaimed as a marvel of inconsistency. Why had he been so exercised at the time by the adverse outcome of a practice game which his men were prepared to win or lose with equal equanimity? Why had the loss of a game of so little moment gnawed and gnawed in his heart?

It had been obvious, as he described Michigan's "workout" with Notre Dame as one of "the worst kind of games to lose," that he was concerned enough to indulge in the pastime of what-might-have-been. He had particular reference to that moot situation in which Notre Dame blocked Captain Allerdice's attempt to place-kick. He was concerned enough to imply agreement with eyewitness Walter Camp's observation. ". . . if the ball had been passed better," the All-American expert said, "and if Michigan's line had held better, it might have been different." If Yost also thought it might have been different had Michigan elected to carry the ball, he had to disdain the precedent record discrediting such an expectation. Throughout the entire game in 1908 and up to this controversial point in the 1909 game, the Wolverines had been unable to pierce the Notre Dame line when it vitally counted. Yes, it might have been different, as the inevitable wag commented, if Michigan had been playing Olivet.

Yost also took this practice game seriously enough to complain that against Michigan Notre Dame had fielded men who had "played many years beyond the limit recognized in the West." Only the graduating Sam Dolan and Red Miller of the 1909 squad were four-year lettermen. No freshmen at all were used. If lineman Luke Kelley and halfback Red Kelly had replaced Dolan and Miller, Notre Dame would not have collapsed. On the other hand, meeting Yost in his own alley, there were those who wondered if a conscientious self-scrutiny of the Michigan eligible roll call, followed by appropriate action, would cost the Wolverines some key performers. At least the possibility was susceptible to Yost's own exaggerated brand of speculation.

Asked for a statement following the Michigan game, Capt. Edwards had capped brief blanket praise for all his mates with the characteristic and significant laconicism: "Marquette next." The surprise close shave of 1908 had rankled for a year. No sooner had Michigan been passed than the players, notwithstanding Coach Longman's declared respect for both Miami and Wabash, hedgehopped mentally to the Thanksgiving special with Marquette at Milwaukee. Their appraisal of the prospectus was vindicated after they disposed of Miami 46-0 and Wabash 38-0 and caught themselves something of a tartar in the Hilltoppers.

For many years I attributed the nip-and-tuck pattern of the early Marquette football rivalry (6-0, Notre Dame; 0-0, 5-5, 0-0) to some kind of jinx as well as to a fighting spirit comparable with Notre Dame's. I also unfairly emphasized the result of the 1912 game, played in Chicago, the fifth and last of a five-game series which Notre Dame won, 69 to 0. As a participant in a Notre Dame victory when football relations were passingly resumed in 1921, I felt that the 21-7 score did not denote adequately the margin of our superiority. It required a recent review of the record from 1908 through 1911 to give me a more competent appreciation of the Hilltoppers' potential as upsetters of the 1909 Western champions.

While holding or tying Notre Dame in that four-year stretch the Marquettes scored 605 points to all-opponents' 52 as they won 18 games, lost 5 and tied 6. Their only games with Western Conference teams resulted in a 6-6 stand-off with Illinois (1908) and close decisions to Wisconsin (6-9, 1908) and Michigan (5-6, 1909). Nevertheless, despite this impressive overall history, I would partly explain the scoreless tie with Notre Dame in 1909 by a number of factors in support of the Hilltoppers' basic merit and their will to win; namely, a grassless, sandy, heavy-footed field; continued absence from the lineup of Billy Ryan, Pete Dwyer and Pete Vaughan; a broken collarbone with which linebacker Sam Dolan played a good part of the game; an unprecedented number of 15-yard penalties for blocking infractions.

The aggregate of these elements lined up against Notre Dame suggests that it took no less than champions just to emerge even with a Marquette whose would-be giant-killers played with the heart of the dauntless namesake of their institution.

This, of course, was not the mood in which the Notre Dame players submitted to this disappointment of their expectation to wind up with an all-victorious slate. They suffered the blues without waiting for Monday just as we did after dropping our championship Thanksgiving game to Goshen, 12-5. Other values being equal, any regrets for the last game of the season dig deepest because you can't redeem this Saturday's frustrations at the expense of next Saturday's opponent. For me our defeat by Goshen was the last game of my first and what might well be my last season of football. This species of total finality aggravated the aching distress with which I reviewed the group reverse and my individual responsibility.

For me the week of the Goshen game had begun on a high note, with a field test of the hypothetical resolution and fortitude with which my witness of the Notre Dame-Wabash affair, garnished by Red Miller's final run, had infused me. Usually, I was on the receiving end of Capt. Mike Kirby's practice punts. In Monday's pre-Goshen workout, I had asked our captain to prescribe live tackling and let me try to do some of it. Lining up to the weakside, as for punt protection, I headed downfield at the snap of the ball. Receiving were fullback Phil Nicar and halfback Frank Whitaker, two of the best runners on the squad, college prospects who would make the grade.

Big Mike's kick was typically far and high. I could see the startled look on Phil's face as I banged into him high on the chest a breath after the ball hit there. It bounced rearward to Whitaker, who slanted upfield to my right. I adjusted laterally. I was so far from the target that a footrace seemed to impend. Neither Whitty nor I reckoned with the reflexes Red Miller had wound up in me with a subconscious trigger. Without thinking I left my feet on a long dive, as if my objective was as vulnerable as our sawdust dummy on Girls' Night. Making contact just below the knees from the side and rear, I laid a good man low and hard. As we got up, Whitaker's face, too, seemed to register slight shock. No wonder. Nobody had ever seen me cutting all strings like that. I felt kite-high myself. No matter that a vigorous straight-arm might have nosed me into the turf. If I should miss a tackle in the Goshen game, and I would, it wouldn't be physical fear that betrayed me. It would be my old bugaboo, the tendency to play too tactically safe. My dynamic recovery from "tackleitis" seemed to invigorate the whole squad.

In my notes I find the fragment of another kind gesture off the typewriter of my friend on the *Times*. It represents that quarterback Grant's play in the Goshen game on Thanksgiving Day was distinguished by his "scoring the five points for South Bend, and by his fast and *heavy* playing, making the longest and most needed gains." Obviously, I didn't make all the gains we needed to win. The italics are mine. My light weight (133 pounds) impels me to suppose that the writer meant "heady," although my most vivid memory of intellectual performance would be of a two-point-bonus bonehead I'll come back to. The heady one on that field was Goshen's chunky quarterback Wiseman, whose reputation for competence and trickery was well known to us in advance. The only sleeper he tried on us, however, backfired. Once, as the teams were lining up for a new scrimmage, he called out sharply, "Give me the ball!" Everybody was standing straight up. His center turned and tossed the ball to Wiseman, who began to pace off yardage to his left in long steps. About 10 yards to the flank he suddenly turned to dash downfield. Under the existing rules the ball was in play. We were supposed to be caught gawking. Because we had been alerted, right end Ken Berkey smashed him for a loss. But Wiseman got two touchdowns out of a team intrinsically inferior to ours, out of which I got none. Our one touchdown resulted from a strictly individual offbeat defensive gambit.

Wiseman is the only Goshenite in that game that I can recall by name. Goshen had a halfback whose name I don't remember but whose game I couldn't forget. Twice he cut back over his left tackle and veered to our right. Twice fullback Phil Nicar nailed him neatly after a short gain. The third time he wrenched free of Phil's clutch. If I missed he was long gone. I should have supported our linebacker closely enough to have reached the runner before he recovered his full stride. The next best thing would have been to make him show by forcing him one way or the other. Instead of acting, I thought; I used my head. (This was what the *Times* man meant by "heavy"?) I used my head to remind myself that to miss this tackle would be fatal. I had to be sure not to miss. All this mental activity was both superfluous and nugatory. I was still thinking when he head-faked to my left and cut to my right, congealing me in my tracks with the feeling that I was trying to move in a dream on lead-weighted feet. Touchdown: Goshen, 5; South Bend, 0.

My trouble was lack of confidence in the capacity of my reflexes to respond to the challenge of the situation without a conscious command. It might have been overcome by specific drills that would have sharpened and pointed my reflexes and built up my reliance on them, an interactionary process. In this same game, in another category of defensive play, I myself would demonstrate the potency of purely reflex reaction, of action uninhibited by thought.

Two factors set me up to act reflexively when I went down under punts. I was automatically relaxed by my release from the mental stresses of responsibility in the safety spot. Confidence in my reflexes to meet the exigencies of this specific area of action had been established in the one rather dramatically successful practice exercise on Monday. I confess that the minimal potential of concussion on a muddy field was another encouraging factor. At any rate, when no rushing pressure developed on my side of punt formation, I sped downfield under one of Mike Kirby's early punts without conscious thought or care, a flesh-and-blood automaton. You might literally say that before I knew it I was letting go at a receiver and hurtling into him waist-high while he was in dead center of a lateral movement.

After that Wiseman appointed himself to check me on punts. I dodged or, when he lunged too low, hurdled him, yelling taunts. The last tackle I made under these conditions pleased me most and has lingered in memory with the greatest clarity. It was not a technically sound tackle. I must have been detained this time; the punt catcher had got well under way and was pointed down the sideline with a clear path ahead. I left the ground like a winged squirrel. This time I made contact just below the knees and a strong straight-arm might have shunted me. As it was, I knocked the runner off his feet and one of my mates made the scene in time to immobilize him. It was legal then and for some time afterwards for a ball carrier grounded outside the grasp of an opponent to rise and shine again.

I'd met this occasion with my full potential. Looking back, I might conjure up other isolated peaks of performance—in baseball and basketball as well as football. That's the story of the average athlete. Consistency is the mark of the great ones.

Mike Kirby got off an exceptionally high and fairly far punt. For some reason no Goshenite tried to impede my progress downfield. This defensive omission enabled me to duplicate the first phase of that practice episode in which I had run through punt-receiver Phil Nicar. Just as the Goshen receiver thought he was catching the ball, I similarly hit him chest-high without losing my feet, recovered the fumble in this instance, and ran the remaining 25 or 30 yards for our only points. Goshen protested that I had illegally outraced the ball to its target, but the official ruled in our favor—not, I know, because he was our man, but because Mul Williams was above ruling against his own in a gratuitous gesture of integrity.

In any case, retribution was not long on the way. First, I think, Goshen scored a second touchdown on a short plunge, capping what precedent sequence or incident I don't remember. Then I contributed two points to Goshen's total of 12 (to our 5, both sides missing points-after) when a Goshen punt stopped, with a final eccentric bounce laterally, on our one-foot line. I picked it up on the run, but Mike Kirby, assuming that it had gone into the end zone, yelled, "Touch it down!" I instinctively did so; but, since I had to cross the goal line to obtain the advantage of the touchback Mike had in mind, I scored a safety for us and two points for them. This, of course, was one of those things that burn and burn, all the worse when inflicted by the superimposition of another's judgment on your own: in a football game or in any other competitive circumstance.

Some athletes can forget a contest as soon as it's over, I've heard or read somewhere. Others rerun it recurrently the rest of their lives, in some proportion to its immediate impact and to the principal's other interests in life. My nature made me replay a game over and over at least until Monday's practice. The Goshen game, a defeat, closing the season and perhaps my football-playing career, hit me especially hard. After eating at the hotel where we had dressed, I was sitting in the lobby by myself, nagged by assorted unhappy memories of my personal performance: the missed tackle giving Goshen a touchdown; the two-point goal-line blunder; my inability in general to get loose on plays from scrimmage (I had never recovered fully from the overexpectations induced by my five-touchdown debut against defenseless La Porte); the particular futility of having lined up in conscious imitation of Red Miller's posture, preparatory to sprinting sensationally around Goshen's right end, only to be flattened ignominiously while still running laterally. It took a traveling salesman, who introduced himself as a fellow Grant, to rescue me temporarily from this fit of self-castigation.

This friendly little man had seen the game, and had followed my play particularly because of the clan name we shared. He put a much higher evaluation on my offensive game than I would, but I wasn't averse to letting him sell me on his superior judgment. In truth, I milked him for praise with the gall of a vaudeville ham, but less obviously with small gestures of self-deprecation. At home on Sunday, though, Gloomy Gus would have been a comparative ultra-optimist. Not even my unprecedented tackling splurge under punts provided more than passing relief from my morbid misery. In the light of later gridiron experience, however, I must grade this defensive display A-plus if only for its rarity in my record.

In 1916 the quarterback at Notre Dame was the deep man in a diamond defense. After the war Knute Rockne switched from the 7-1-2-1 to the 7-2-2, but I still played a mental safety. I never thought of going downfield under punts. The Goshen game stands out uniquely in my memoirs because that day I tackled again and again with fierce, controlled and joyous abandon—thanks to the encouragement of a rain-softened field and the inspiration of the time I saw Notre Dame's champions of the West in game action, high-lighted for me by a red-headed halfback from the town of my birth.

15

All that is what Notre Dame and football meant to this youth the year before the time of Knute Rockne. I made a basketball letter by the end of the first school term and the termination of my athletic eligibility as a midyear potential graduate. I continued in school in order to be graduated in June with the 1910 class, and to defer the dread day when I would be expected to go to work. Our class prophetess wrote for *The Interlude*, "Chester Grant will coach at Yale." But a more immediate if borrowed distinction awaited me. Shortly before commencement, the city editor of the South Bend *Times* sent for me to cover Central League baseball. Only two or three years earlier this assignment had belonged to a colorful character who was making his mark with the Chicago *Tribune*. He must have covered fires, too, as I would do—the Central Station firemen all had known Ring Lardner. Somehow around midsummer I contracted a case of jaundice or something that enabled me to enjoy a segment of the usual summer vacation with the grandparents in Defiance. I recuperated while driving a grocery wagon for a vacationing delivery man. That year the focus of our interest in the Central League had been shifted from South Bend to Evansville, where my uncle had taken over the operation with my father as club secretary. Meantime, the Benders, under new management, were bidding for the pennant and I would return to South Bend in time to cover the final drive for the South Bend

Tribune; also an exhibition game with the world champion Philadelphia Athletics.

When the 1910 football season opened I was getting out the *Tribune* sports columns in addition to covering undertakers, Central Fire Station, Y.M.C.A., Chamber of Commerce, the high school principal's office and miscellaneous sources of news and information. I revived my dual role of 1909 for one occasion by quarterbacking the alumni pickups in the annual game with the high school team and then editing the high school correspondent's story.

Our Notre Dame correspondent in 1910 was a friend, varsity miler Fred Steers of Chicago. Along with his teammates Fred had officiated when I took part in our interclass meet in the Big Gym and the Northern Indiana competition on Cartier Field. He had shown a special interest in my efforts. After the 100-yard final he had come into the dressing room all smiles to tell me that two of three watches had clocked me at 10 seconds. The third timing of 10⅕ was official, but I never ran that fast again, at least in recorded time, and for my own private record I recognized the 10-flat mark. The one-fifth second might represent as much as two yards of distance covered; if this discrepancy disturbed my conscience, I dismissed the qualm as scrupulosity.

But the pertinence here of my relationship with Fred Steers is concerned with my introduction to a football candidate who would become known as the most famous football coach. Fred Steers and I, of course, didn't dream that we were handling a potential historic document the Monday morning that he laid on my desk the story of an early-season game containing the following unimpressive sentence:

"Rokne [sic], a freshman, made a good showing at fullback but showed a tendency to fumble."